Thomas Cook

AVELLERS

TURKEY

y
DIANA DARKE

Written by Diana Darke
Updated by Diana Darke
Original photography by Dario Mitidieri
Updated photography by Lindsay and Pete Bennett

Editing and page layout by Cambridge Publishing Management Ltd,
Unit 2, Burr Elm Court, Caldecote CB23 7NU
Series Editor: Karen Beaulah

Published by Thomas Cook Publishing
A division of Thomas Cook Tour Operations Ltd.
Company Registration No. 1450464 England

PO Box 227, The Thomas Cook Business Park,
Coningsby Road, Peterborough PE3 8SB, United Kingdom
E-mail: books@thomascook.com
www.thomascookpublishing.com
Tel: +44 (0)1733 416477

ISBN: 978-1-84157-709-8

Text © 2007 Thomas Cook Publishing
Maps © 2007 Thomas Cook Publishing

First edition © 2005 Thomas Cook Publishing
Second edition © 2007 Thomas Cook Publishing

Project Editor: Sasha Heseltine
Production/DTP Editor: Steven Collins

Printed and bound in Italy by: Printer Trento.

Cover design by: Liz Lyons Design, Oxford
Front cover credits: © Thomas Cook, © Inter Vision Ltd/Pictures Colour
Library, © Thomas Cook
Back cover credits: © Thomas Cook, © Thomas Cook

Contents

KEY TO MAPS

☆ Start of drive, walk or boat trip

✈ Airport   — railway line

▪ Public building   – motorway

ℹ Tourist Information   - - - ferry route

Introduction

Turkey is a remarkable passage-land between Europe and Asia, and the country reflects these two identities. The western half, with the cities of Istanbul, Izmir and Antalya, is richer and more densely populated, looking towards Europe and the Mediterranean. The other part, heading from Ankara eastwards, with its rugged, haunting steppelands of Anatolia, points more towards Turkey's Asian heritage.

It is to the western part that most visitors come, drawn by the legendary magic of Istanbul and by the longest and cleanest coastline in the Mediterranean. Eastern Turkey remains a different story, being more suited to the adventurer than the beach-lover. The dignity of the Turkish people will

Turkey

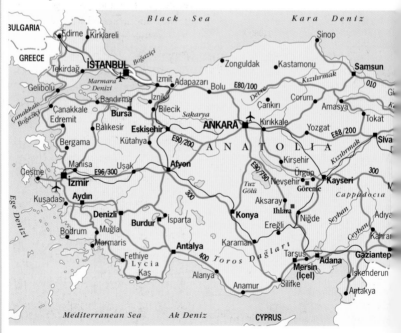

THOMAS COOK'S TURKEY

Visits to Turkey by Thomas Cook tourists began soon after he had established his Egyptian business in 1869.

By 1877 Constantinople (Istanbul) had become an essential part of a Middle East tour and Cook passengers on the Orient Express were soon added to those who embarked here for Alexandria.

Further tours were added as the Wagons-Lits Company extended its services to Smyrna (Izmir). By 1913 Thomas Cook was advertising such exotic tours as Mount Ararat by rail. In more recent times, Thomas Cook have promoted holidays at Turkish seaside resorts, city breaks to Istanbul and *gület* cruises.

A boat moored at Kekova harbour

Introduction

impress a first-time visitor. The low price and high quality of food and drink will also please. In terms of

ancient remains, both western and eastern Turkey offer a wealth verging on superfluity, with archaeological sites reaching back to the Stone Age and the Hittites, through Greek and Roman cities, to Byzantine, Seljuk and Ottoman monuments. Many are in magnificent settings. Natural wonders are everywhere – caves, waterfalls, canyons, volcanoes, lakes and springs, with some of the most stunning mountain scenery in the world.

The land

'For once seen, never can the magnificent sight of the "Queen of the Cities" rising out of the sparkling waters of the Bosporus be forgotten, with its seven hills crowned with great domed mosques surrounded by tapering minarets, with marble palaces, built in tiers down to the water's edge of the Sea of Marmara and Golden Horn…'

Lady Dorina Neave, *1890*

Landscape and topography

Modern Turkey is a country with an area of 779,452sq km (300,948sq miles), six times that of Greece, yet with half the number of people per square kilometre. The population is estimated at around 69 million. The Anatolian peninsula has strongly defined geographical limits: the Kara Deniz (Black Sea) to the north; the Aegean in the west and the Mediterranean in the south; and the high mountain ranges that culminate in Büyükağrı Dağı (Mount Ararat) at 5,165m (16,946ft),

A typical landscape – bleak and harsh

to the east. The 5 per cent that lies west of the Çanakkale Boğaziçi (Dardanelles) is flatter, geographically a part of Europe, and contains the cities of Istanbul and Edirne. Its limit is defined by an artificial border whose exact position has varied considerably according to the politics of the day.

The main land mass consists of the bleak steppelands of the central Anatolian Plateau, set at 1,000m (3,300ft), ringed by the verdant Pontic mountains to the north and the Toros (Taurus) to the south. These ranges run east to west and join up with the vast, inhospitable mountainous region in the east that borders Iran and Iraq.

Volcanoes and earthquakes

There are several large volcanoes in Turkey besides Mount Ararat, the highest, but none is thought to be still active. Fault lines do still have movement, and earthquakes in the north and west of Turkey have been common throughout history and continue to strike every ten years or so, the last being in 2000. Both the Boğaziçi (Bosporus) and the Dardanelles owe their existence to the shifting fault lines, and the whole of the Black Sea was created as a result of subsidence along a series of fissures.

Lakes and rivers

This rugged topography has created many lakes, far more than anywhere else in the region. Van Gölü (Lake Van) is the largest, seven times bigger than Lake Geneva. Turkey also boasts the sources of the Dicle (Tigris), 2,800km (1,740 miles) long, and the Fırat (Euphrates), 1,900km (1,180 miles) long.

Climate

The fertile coastal lowlands contrast dramatically with the mountainous interior, and this can lead to enormous seasonal variations in temperature. In the east, winter temperatures can go as low as –40°C (–40°F) with snow lying for 120 days of the year, while the Aegean coastal regions have mild rainy winters and summer temperatures average around 35°C (95°F). Rainfall is highest along the Black Sea Coast.

The land

Ruins such as this ancient mosque can be seen all over the countryside

History

7500 BC	First Stone Age settlements at Çatalhüyük.
1900–1300 BC	Hittite Empire with Hattuflafl (Boğazkale) as capital, contemporary with ancient Egypt and Babylon.
1250 BC	The Trojan War. Fall of Troy (Truva).
1200–700 BC	Migration of Greeks to the Aegean coastal regions. Kingdoms of Phrygia, Ionia, Lycia, Lydia, Caria and Pamphylia. Urartian civilisation in eastern Anatolia.

The Military Museum Band dressed in bright traditional uniforms

700 BC	Birth of Homer in Smyrna (Izmir). Beginnings of Hellenistic culture in Aegean Turkey.
546 BC	Cyrus the Great of Persia invades. Anatolia under Persian rule.
334 BC	Alexander the Great conquers Anatolia, freeing it from the Persians.
130 BC	Anatolia becomes the Roman province of Asia with its capital at Ephesus (Efes).
40 BC	Antony and Cleopatra marry at Antioch.
AD 47–57	St Paul's missionary journeys. First Christian community at Antioch.
313	Christianity accepted as official religion by the Roman Empire.
330	Byzantium renamed Constantinople by Emperor Constantine as capital of Eastern Roman Empire.
527–65	Reign of Justinian and the height of Byzantine power.

1071–1243	Seljuk Turks conquer Anatolia with Konya as their capital.
1096–1204	The Crusades, with Latin armies entering Anatolia for the first time. Byzantine Empire dismembered.
1288	Birth of Ottoman Empire with capital at Bursa.
1453	Mehmet II conquers Constantinople and renames it Istanbul as capital of Ottoman Empire.
1520–66	Reign of Süleyman the Magnificent and the Golden Age of the Ottoman Empire.
1682–1725	Reign of Peter the Great in Russia begins new phase of Russo-Turkish rivalry.
1854	Crimean War. Ottomans are supported by British and French against Russia.
1909	Abdul Hamid, last Ottoman sultan, deposed by the Young Turks.
1914	Turkey enters World War I as ally of Germany. On defeat, the Allies propose a carve-up of the Ottoman Empire.
1915	Gallipoli Campaign. Allied landings on Turkish soil are repulsed.
1919	Atatürk leads Turkish resistance in fight for national sovereignty.
1923	Turkish state proclaimed with Atatürk as President. Exchange of minority populations between Greece and Turkey. Reforms to modernise and secularise the state. Islam disestablished, Arabic script replaced by Latin alphabet, Turkish language revived. Women's veils and the fez banned.
1938	Atatürk dies.
1939–45	Turkey remains neutral in World War II.
1946	Turkey becomes a charter member of United Nations.

NAME CHANGES

The name 'Anatolia', meaning the Asiatic part of modern Turkey, the Asian heartland, comes from the Greek word for east. Under the Romans this area was referred to as Asia Minor.

The city of Istanbul was originally called Byzantium when it was founded in 667 BC, then renamed Constantinople by the Byzantines, before being renamed Istanbul by the Ottomans.

1952	Turkey joins NATO.
1960	Almost bloodless military coup followed by successive inefficient governments.
1964	Turkey becomes associate member of the EU.
1974	Turkey intervenes in Cyprus to protect the Turkish Cypriot community, seizing the northern third of the island.

Obelisk base, Istanbul Hippodrome

1980	Bloodless military coup takes place under General Kenan Evren.
1983	Return to civilian rule.
1984	Resurgence of Kurdish struggle for independence.
1990s	Short-term coalition governments weaken political stability. Large-scale financial mismanagement and rampant inflation almost break the domestic economy. The IMF is called in to help.
	Crackdown by the Turkish military on the Kurds brings accusations of human-rights abuse that weaken Turkey's chance of joining the EU.
1999	The Kurds announce they are ending their campaign of violence.
2003–6	Series of terrorist bombings in Istanbul, Aegean and Mediterranean resorts, aimed at banks, hotels and restaurants with western interests.
2005	New Turkish Lira currency introduced as six zeros are stripped off the old lira.

Lycian tombs carved into the rock face at Dalyan

EU accession negotiations are launched, but without any guarantee of eventual membership.

2006 Turkey sends troops to Lebanon as part of UN Peacekeeping Force.

Pope visits Istanbul and prays in Blue Mosque.

End 2006 Turks cool in their relations with Europe. There is mutual ambivalence towards EU membership talks.

The Ottoman Empire 1326–1922

View from the Topkapı Palace in Istanbul

The Ottomans began as a small tribe of nomadic Turks and ended up as the power that overthrew the Byzantine Empire, dominating the region for the next 600 years. The name Ottoman, Turkish Osmanlı, is derived from their first leader Osman Gazi.

Their first capital was at Bursa in 1326, but their expansion suffered a severe setback when the Mongols under Tamerlane invaded from Central Asia in 1402. They recovered, and by 1453, under Sultan Mehmet II, they took Constantinople after a seven-week siege. Mehmet, thereafter called the Conqueror, began repairing the siege damage, and by 1470 had built the Topkapı Sarayı (Topkapı Palace) as the new imperial residence and

Overview of Topkapı Palace

Türbe of Süleyman the Magnificent in Istanbul

completed the huge Fatih Camii, Mosque of the Conqueror, the first mosque complex of its kind. Mehmet also repopulated the city, bringing in Turks, Greeks, Armenians and Spanish Jews. By the end of the 15th century, Istanbul, as the Turks now called it, was the thriving prosperous capital of an empire. Under Selim the Grim, the empire was extended to Persia, Syria and Egypt. He was preparing a great campaign against Europe when he died unexpectedly in 1520.

The Ottoman Empire reached its peak under Selim's son, Süleyman, known in the west as 'The Magnificent'. Vienna was his only military failure, saving Europe from further Ottoman expansion. He used the booty, tribute and taxes from his conquered territories to adorn Istanbul with charitable institutions and mosque complexes, the grandest of which is the Süleymaniye.

The long, slow decline of the Ottoman Empire started in 1566 with Süleyman's son, Selim II, known as 'The Sot'. Much of the decline is laid at the door of the harems, and historians refer to this period as 'the Rule of the Women', with a succession of ambitious wives and mothers distracting the sultans from affairs of state with sensual pleasures. Civil unrest further weakened the empire and it became known as 'The Sick Man of Europe', losing many of its territories. A disastrous alliance with Germany in World War I finished it off completely.

Politics

Not shaped by any imperialist power, the modern Turkish state has evolved from its own Ottoman legacy. Since the 1920s it has had 59 governments, many of them coalitions, which have grappled with the complex problems arising from the gradual breakdown of the Ottoman administrative and military systems.

The Turkish Republic

When Atatürk wrote the Republican constitution in the late 1920s, he was very specific in his separation of religion from politics. Numerous safeguards were put in place to guard against religious interference, many of which became antiquated and over-zealous as the modern Turkey developed. The ultimate sanction was for the army to step in to protect the constitution, which they did in bloodless military takeovers of government in 1960, 1971, 1980 and 1982. On a more mundane level, countless political parties have been banned over the years, many with little desire to re-establish Islam but simply to provide better representation for the Turkish working and agricultural classes.

Recent events

The 1990s were dark days for Turkish politics. Governments came and went, seemingly unable to take control of an economy that was in meltdown by the end of the decade. Inflation was rising to 90 per cent per annum; the Turkish Lira was in freefall and international investment leached away. At the end of the decade, the International Monetary Fund was called in to rescue the country with a short, sharp shock plan.

The 2002 elections

The November 2002 elections changed the face of Turkish politics. The Justice and Development Party (AKP) won, but they were led by Recep Tayip Erdogan, a man who had been jailed in 1999 for so-called 'anti-secular activities' and was therefore banned from standing in the ballots. Initially a caretaker Prime Minister was appointed, but *vox pop* insisted that Erdogan take up his rightful position and the constitution was amended to allow him to become Prime Minister in March 2003.

Atatürk's fears have not been realised, however. Erdogan has no intention of returning Turkey to its Ottoman past.

His main aim is to strengthen the country's economy, principally through long-term ties with Europe. As part of an agreement to meet EU accession protocols, the institutionalised influence of the military has been restricted. The IMF plan has also been fully implemented, bringing stability to the Turkish Lira and to inflation, which was down to an annual rate of 16 per cent by mid-2003.

Success of the AKP

In the 1980s the Turkish government saw Communism as a threat and made concessions in the teaching of religion. The generations who have grown up with increased access to religious teaching are now the politically active and have developed into a new Islamic middle class not seen before in Turkey, who embrace both a firm (not militant) faith and 'western' attitude to economics.

The future

Turkey remains the only secular democracy in the Muslim world, and its army is the second largest in NATO after the US. The biggest question facing its future is whether EU accession talks stumble on, or whether the country begins to turn its back on Europe in favour of its eastern neighbours. Either way, both politically and economically, Turkey is in a stronger position now under Erdogan than it has been for years.

A photograph taken in 1923 of President Atatürk, popularly known as the 'Father of the Turks'

Culture

Modern Turks are descendants of the Turkish tribes from Central Asia who entered Anatolia during the 11th to 13th centuries and interbred with the ancient native stock of the region. Although the Turks were converted to Islam during these centuries, their distinctive language and popular culture makes them identifiably separate from the rest of the Muslim world. Immigrants from Balkan countries also play a substantial role in the nation's life. There is a sizeable Kurdish population, around ten per cent, which is primarily located in the southeast.

Character

As a people the Turks are distinguished by their dignity, nobility, honesty, great physical endurance and courage. The Turkish character is one of contrasts: they are hardworking yet realise the futility of hurry and worry; serious, yet cherish a comic character as their favourite folklore hero; they respect the authority of the state, yet insist on democracy; they can be ruthless, yet kind and hospitable. Many are poor yet they often disdain money. Turks mean what they say. There is no deviousness in the Turkish character, and you will be told a straightforward 'no' if something you have asked for is not possible, rather than fobbed off with empty promises and assurances.

Turks despise what they see as a lack of control: it does not pay to lose your temper with a Turk, for it achieves nothing and merely earns you contempt.

The Turks are extremely proud of their country and its past, and Atatürk's slogan *Ne mutlu Türküm diyene* ('How happy is he who can say he is a Turk') is blazoned on hillsides and strung on banners on public holidays. Military service is extremely tough and is compulsory for 18 months. It is also regarded by most as an important educational experience, teaching the illiterate to read and write and instructing them in a trade. Turkish officers, drawn from the middle and lower classes, regard themselves as the nation's élite and its social conscience.

Honour and virility are the two most highly prized qualities, and Turkey is still an essentially male society. In a Turkish prison, the thief is the lowest form of life, while the murderers are the élite. Motives for murder are generally to do with honour, and therefore respected.

The influence of Islam remains strong, and beads to ward off the evil eye can still be seen in most cars and taxis. Alcohol is consumed in moderation and public drunkenness is unheard of. Young Turks are very keen to be educated, and the Turkish workforce is highly educated, with a higher number of graduates per capita than some northern European countries. The quality of education remains unevenly spread, with the already favoured western areas receiving the lion's share of teachers and resources at the expense of the provincial east.

Country versus city

The gulf between the rich and poor in Turkey is noticeable, particularly as you travel further east. About 40 per cent of the country's workforce is engaged in agriculture and lives in rural areas, while the remainder work in heavy industry and manufacturing in the city factories. In recent years the trend has been towards urban migration, with the rural poor searching for better lifestyles in the city. This has led to the growth of vast shanty suburbs round the main cities of Istanbul, Ankara, Izmir and Adana. With this agricultural-industrial balance, Turkey is unusually self-sufficient, in food and in manufacturing, and its pride in this is almost tangible. Oil is its only serious deficiency, as it produces less than 20 per cent of its needs.

The country has vast potential for economic development, but so far mismanagement and fear of disturbing the vested interests of a powerful élite have held it back from realising this potential.

Cotton pickers at a plantation

Festivals and events

Turkey offers a wide range of festivals, fairs and shows, from celebrations of music, art, drama and dance to the more unusual spectacles of the Sufi Whirling Dervishes and camel wrestling.

January

Camel wrestling Aydın. For most of the month. This unusual 'sport' involves two male camels pushing and shoving each other. While vicious, it is not usually a fight to the death.

May

Ephesus Festival of Culture and Tourism Roman theatre of Ephesus. Folk dancing, concerts and plays. (*See also p69.*)

May–June

Ankara International Arts Festival This is held to promote Turkey on an international level, with Turkish art, traditional Turkish classical music and Turkish folklore music.

June

Pergamum Festival Asklepieion theatre. Plays and folk dancing.
International Wine Competition Ürgüp. 7–13 June.
Music and Art Festival Marmaris.

TURKISH MUSIC AND DANCE

The lively Turkish folk music that originated on the steppes of Asia is in complete contrast to the refined Turkish classical music of the Ottoman court. Distinct also from the folk music is the Ottoman military music performed by the Janissary band in Istanbul, played with kettle drums, clarinets, cymbals and bells.

Each region in Turkey has its own special folk dance and costume. In the Black Sea region, for example, is the 'Horon' dance, performed by men only, dressed in black with silver trimmings.

The Sword and Shield Dance of Bursa represents the Ottoman conquest of the city, performed by men in early Ottoman battle dress.

The well-known Spoon Dance is performed from Konya to Silifke by colourfully dressed men and women with a pair of wooden spoons in each hand.

Artvin Kafkasör Culture and Art Festival. Last week of June. Bullfights on the Kafkasör plateau. Folk dancing and wrestling.

June–July

Bursa International Culture and Art Festival 12 June–12 July. Folk dancing and music.

Istanbul International Art and Culture Festival 20 June–30 July. This festival displays the full range of the country's dance, art and music.

July

Akşehir Nasreddin Hoca Festival 5–10 July. In honour of the famous wit, with plays of his anecdotes and plenty of folk dancing.

Ceramic Festival Kütahya.

August

Samsun Fair and Folkdance Festival 1–25 August.

Çanakkale Troy Festival 15–18 August. There is a variety of folk dances, music, and tours of Mount Ida and Troy.

Folk dancers dressed in traditional costumes in Istanbul

August–September

Izmir International Fair 20 August–20 September. Amusements fair with cultural and commercial exhibitions. The city's hotels are packed and it is best to avoid them during this month.

September

Bodrum Culture and Art Week 1–9 September. Concerts in Bodrum Castle, local craft exhibits and water-sports shows.

Cappadocia Festival 21–25 September. Grape harvest celebration and folk dancing.

Mersin Fashion and Textile Show 15 September–5 October. With music and folklore.

October

Antalya Film and Art Festival Some performances are held in the Roman theatre at Aspendos.

Republic Day 29 October. To commemorate the proclamation of the republic by Atatürk in 1923. Parades in the cities.

December

St Nicholas Festival Demre/Kale. 6–8 December.

Mevlana Festival Konya. 9–17 December. Hotels are packed for this, the only occasion in the year when the Whirling Dervishes can be seen performing (*see pp126–7*).

Camel wrestling Aydın, especially at Germencik. Continues throughout December and January.

Impressions

'The Turk is unusually full of contradictions. Not only has he East and West in him, European and Asian, but an intense pride combined with an acute inferiority complex, a deep xenophobia with an overwhelming hospitality to strangers, a profound need for flattery with an absolute disregard for what anybody thinks of him.'

David Hotham, *Times correspondent, 1975*

Body language

Turks say 'no' (*hayır* or *yok*) by lifting the head backwards, a gesture easily mistaken for yes.

Turks say 'yes' (*evet*) by nodding the head down.

Shake your head from side to side to signify you do not understand.

Finger pointing, public nose-blowing, public kissing or hugging of the opposite sex are considered offensive. An overfirm handshake is thought impolite.

Women should avoid too much eye contact with male strangers as this can be misread as encouragement instead of normal social behaviour. Western pornography and films have done much to foster the view that Western women are 'available'. Women walking alone or even in pairs late at night are regarded as inviting male attention.

Crime and security

The crime rate is very low. It is, in fact, far lower than in Western countries, although pickpocketing and petty theft have increased since the advent of tourism. Beware of these dangers, especially in crowded centres like the Kapalıçarşı (Covered Bazaar) of Istanbul. Horror stories of Westerners being clapped in prison only apply to those who are found carrying drugs or who have seriously infringed the law in some way.

Never risk photography when it is expressly forbidden by a notice. Travel in Turkey is safe and unrestricted, especially since the ceasefire with the Kurds opened up the east, but extra

Taking a rest outside the Fatih Camii, Istanbul

12

Thursday

DONNERSTAG | JEUDI

July

JULI | JUILLET

(UK) Battle of the Boyne Day
(Northern Ireland only)

Gustav Stickley, Oak sideboard for Craftsman Workshops, c. 1902–1903

vigilance is called for in the wake of the terrorist bombings in Istanbul and tourist resorts aimed at hotels and restaurants with Western interests.

Driving

Traffic drives on the right so all cars are left-hand drive. Driving habits and styles are less disciplined than western Europe or North America, but relatively orderly compared to most Middle Eastern countries. Pedestrian crossings are a rarity and the driver always has right of way over the pedestrian. Signposting is good and road conditions are generally fine, though potholes are a regular feature east of Ankara.

Getting around

In Istanbul, car hire would be a mistake, as there are so many taxis on the streets that are both cheaper and easier, saving you the headache of navigation. Taxis are all metered and tipping is not usual. Outside Istanbul it is definitely best to hire a car, as so many interesting places in Turkey lie off the main roads. If funds cannot run to this, the bus is the next best, and all major cities and towns in Turkey are linked by excellent cheap and efficient bus services, clean and air-conditioned. Hitch-hiking is possible but not that common, and is not advisable for women alone (*see also pp180–81 & 186–7*).

Language

English and German are widely spoken and understood, especially in the big cities and in the Aegean and Mediterranean tourist centres. Turks learn English as their first foreign language at school. Lack of Turkish is therefore not a problem unless you are travelling in remoter or eastern parts (*see p182*). Since Atatürk in the 1920s,

Road conditions are good in the cities, such as Kuşadasi

Atatürk: Islam in a secular state

Turkey is unique in the Muslim world as a model of a multi-party democracy. Religion is divorced from government and affairs of state, and this can be credited to one man, Kemal Atatürk, 'Father of the Turks' (1881–1938). A military hero, he organised the growing Turkish nationalist movement into a concerted rejection of the Allies' proposed carve-up of the Ottoman Empire. His efforts were crowned by the 1923 Treaty of Lausanne which recognised Turkish sovereignty over what are approximately its present-day borders (see p14).

During the remaining 15 years of his life Atatürk carried out a series of far-reaching reforms designed to westernise Turkey and integrate it into the modern world. He terminated the caliphate, exiled the sultan, abolished the Ministry of Religious Affairs, disbanded religious orders, sequestrated religious property and forbade religious instruction. In 1928 Islam was disestablished and the constitution proclaimed Turkey a secular state.

Atatürk did not oppose religion itself, merely its interference in government. He held that everyone could be a devout Muslim in his private life, but that politics was a separate matter for public debate. In modern Turkey politicians find this a difficult line to follow, as they recognise the power of Islam, particularly in the countryside.

Atatürk on horseback, Ankara

The blue-eyed 'Father of the Turks' and the Turkish flag

At election time, therefore, there is invariably some pandering to religious traditionalism to secure the rural vote.

Among the people themselves the country-city divide endures, and city-dwelling Turks tend to be low-key about their adherence to Islam. In the villages, religion still plays an important role, but there is nothing like the wave of fundamentalism that some alarmist media reports like to imagine.

The memory of Atatürk is everywhere – his portrait hangs in every public place, his statue stands in every town square and his face is on all stamps and banknotes.

Atatürk Monument, Taksim Square, Istanbul

Turkish has used the Latin alphabet (like English), with just a few extra symbols like *umlauts* (¨) to cope with different vowel sounds. Turkish is a Ural-Altaic language unrelated to European languages or to Arabic. It has an extremely complex grammar.

Islam

The word Islam itself means 'submission' in Arabic, and Muslims are those who submit themselves to Allah, the One True God, who is the same God as in Christianity and Judaism. The sacred book of Islam is the Koran, which was revealed by divine inspiration through the Prophet Muhammad. Muhammad was not divine, he was the last of the prophets. Jesus Christ is recognised as a prophet but not as divine. This is a major point on which Islam diverges from Christianity, Muslims viewing the Christian Holy Trinity as heretical and as infringing the oneness of God. The Five Pillars or essential duties of Islam are, first, to declare the creed 'There is no god but God and Muhammad is the messenger of God', second is to pray five times a day, third is to pay the *zakat*, or alms tax, fourth is to fast in Ramadan, and fifth is to visit Mecca at least once in a lifetime.

Calls to prayer

You will hear these broadcast by loudspeaker from the minarets, and they can sound enchanting in large cities where all the mosques start

The courtyard of the Blue Mosque

within moments of each other.

The call to prayer is sung in a ritualised chant, a much-prized art which the *muezzin* (the caller) takes years to perfect. Muslims pray five times a day: at dawn, at midday, mid-afternoon, sunset and before bed. The Friday noon prayer is the essential congregational prayer, when mosques are full. During prayers the believers must face Mecca, a direction indicated by the prayer niche (*mihrab*) in each mosque.

Mosque etiquette

Before stepping on a mosque's carpets, always remove your shoes and leave them in the racks provided outside. Women should wear a scarf to cover their hair. Avoid visiting mosques on Fridays or at prayer times. Most large city mosques close to non-Muslims from noon till 1pm for noonday prayers.

Ramadan

This is the Muslim month of fasting when, in certain places such as holy cities like Konya, visitors may experience difficulty getting food and drink during daylight hours. Ramadan is a moveable feast following the lunar calendar, so the date changes every year. Muslims fast from dawn to dusk, then break the fast each evening with large amounts of feasting and celebrating, which continue late into the night. Children, pregnant women, the old and the sick, and people who are on long journeys are exempted from the fast. The test of willpower is especially tough on the women, who have to continue to prepare meals for the children and elderly during the day, then have to prepare

MOSQUE GEOGRAPHY

imaret	soup kitchen attached to mosque for feeding the poor.
medrese	theological school attached to a mosque.
mihrab	prayer niche in wall of mosque that faces Mecca.
minbar	pulpit from which sermons are preached.
türbe	mausoleum.

Impressions

the main evening feast for the men. The exact age at which children have to start fasting remains a matter of individual choice, but is generally after eight.

In Istanbul and the Aegean and Mediterranean regions, restaurants remain open as usual during Ramadan and visitors would barely notice anything different. In the east it is more strictly observed and many restaurants will shut during the day, while only a few of the bigger hotels continue to serve alcohol.

Religious devotion in the Eyüp Camii, Istanbul's holiest mosque

Gülets on the water take tourists for a seaside view

The Sunni/Shia divide

Ninety-nine per cent of Turks are Sunni Muslims, which is the conservative orthodox majority, following the '*Sunna*' or trodden path. The Sunni/Shia divide is the major sectoral split in Islam, as the Protestant/Catholic split is in Christianity. The divide dates back to the years immediately after Muhammad's death in 632 when the Shia supported Muhammad's son-in-law Ali and his descendants as the true successors, while the Sunnis believed the succession should be decided by the Islamic clergy. The Shia are the more outspoken element today, but account for only ten per cent of Muslims worldwide. Most are to be found in Iran, Iraq, Pakistan and India.

Itineraries

Turkey lends itself very well to touring holidays and visitors. When planning more detailed visits, remember that museums are invariably shut on Mondays throughout the country. The following are feasible two-week itineraries, assuming you have your own transport and that you are returning to the same airport. Some companies allow you to hire a car at one airport and return it at another, which obviously allows a lot more flexibility. If you are using public transport, the same itinerary can take a few days longer.

Tour 1

Istanbul (3 days), Bursa, Troy (Truva), Pergamum, Kuşadası, Ephesus (Efes),

Priene, Miletos (Milet), Didyma, Bodrum (2 days), Pamukkale (2 days), Sardis (Sardes), Izmir, Balıkesir, Iznik, Istanbul.

Tour 2
Izmir, Kuşadası, Ephesus, Priene, Miletos, Didyma, Bodrum (2 days), Marmaris (2 days), Fethiye, Kalkan, Kaş, Antalya, Pamukkale (2 days), Izmir.

Tour 3
Antalya, Perge, Aspendos, Side (2 days), Alanya, Anamur, Silifke,

Ürgüp (3 days), Konya (2 days), Eğirdir, Antalya.

Tour 4
Ankara (2 days), Boğazkale, Amasya, Sivas, Divriği, Elazığ, Diyarbakır, Şanlı Urfa, Nemrut Dağı, Adana, Ürgüp (2 days), Ankara.

Tour 5
Trabzon (2 days), Artvin, Kars, Ani, Doğubayazıt, Van (2 days), Diyarbakır, Mardin, Nemrut Dağı, Malatya, Erzincan, Erzurum, Sumela, Trabzon.

Impressions

The minaret of a former sultan's palace reaches for the sky

Istanbul

Here is one of the world's most magical and evocative cities, viewed by the West as the gateway to the East with all its tantalising promise. It is not European, nor Asian, nor Middle Eastern, but has flavours of all three. The only city to stand astride two continents, Istanbul's unique location lies at the heart of its magic. Europe is separated from Asia by the hilly straits of the Boğaziçi (Bosporus), and different parts of the European city are separated by the inlet of the Haliç (Golden Horn), one of the world's most sheltered harbours. This abundance of water is Istanbul's other special charm.

It has been the capital of three world empires, the Roman, the Byzantine and the Ottoman, and has borne three names – Byzantium, Constantinople and Istanbul. For nearly 1,000 years it was the most important city in the Western and near-Eastern worlds.

Political power moved to Ankara in 1923, along with all the government ministries and embassies, leaving Istanbul for the first time in 16 centuries without the status of capital of an empire. But for all that, Istanbul remains Turkey's cultural and commercial capital, generating some 40 per cent of the gross national product.

The city has doubled its population every 15 years since 1950 because of immigration from the countryside. The 2005 census revealed a population in excess of 12 million people. Its infrastructure, not surprisingly, has been unable to keep pace, and there is terrific pressure on roads and services.

There are sprawling dormitory suburbs, unplanned and unsightly, though the average visitor will be blissfully unaware of them.

LANDMARKS

Some parts of the city make excellent landmarks and so help orient the visitor.

Ayasofya and Sultanahmet Camii (Blue Mosque)

Ayasofya has four minarets and the Blue Mosque has six, the obvious difference when viewed from a distance.

The whole precinct from Ayasofya to the Topkapı Sarayı (Topkapı Palace) and from Ayasofya to the Blue Mosque is pedestrianised, and makes pleasant strolling, especially since the addition of carefully landscaped gardens.

Apart from these three great monuments, this hub of the city has many smaller places of interest. In front of the Blue Mosque is the Hippodrome, which was the ancient sports and civic centre of Byzantium. Chariot races and circuses were held here, and the total capacity has been estimated at 100,000 spectators. The obelisk here is only the upper third of the original, which broke during shipment from Egypt. (*Also see pp32–3 & p39.*)

Beyoğlu

Beyoğlu is the quaint 19th-century European city, much of which has been turned into a pedestrian precinct. Most embassies and consulates are based here.

Bosporus and its two bridges

The Bosporus is the strait that separates Europe from Asia (*see pp56–7*). The first bridge, built in 1973, is called Boğaziçi Köprüsü, and the second, completed in 1988, in an attempt to relieve traffic congestion on the first, is called Fatih Sultan Mehmet Köprüsü. It spans the straits further north between the famous fortresses of Rumeli Hisar and Anadolu Hisar, the same place where the Persian Emperor Darius built his bridge of boats in 512 BC.

A pedestrian street in Beyoğlu

GETTING AROUND ISTANBUL

The best way to get around in Istanbul is to walk whenever possible and to catch taxis or ferries when not. It is not worth hiring a car, as parking is always tricky, and you will waste a lot of time getting lost.

Bozdoğan Kemeri (Aqueduct of Valens)

A huge two-tier structure, this is an imposing landmark that spans Atatürk Bulvarı (Atatürk Boulevard), linking Istanbul's third and fourth hills. It was built by the Emperor Valens in AD 375.

Column of Constantine

A porphyry column standing between the Grand Bazaar and the Çemberlitaş Baths, it is the oldest remnant of Roman Byzantium and was erected in AD 330 by Constantine as a dedication to the city.

Divan Yolu

The Divan Yolu is the main road along the top of the hills of old Istanbul, linking the Covered Bazaar area of Beyazıt to the Sultanahmet district. A modern tram now runs along it, and much of it is pedestrianised.

Eminönü Meydanı (Eminönü Square)

This bustling square, below the Topkapı, where the Galata Köprüsü (bridge) spans the Golden Horn, is considered the heart of the city. The boat stations are all here, as is the railway station, Sirkeci.

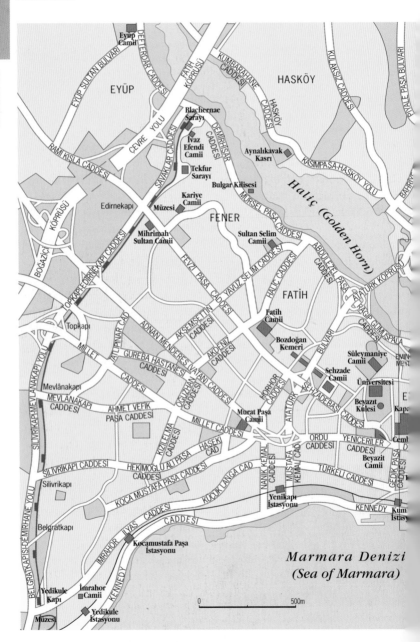

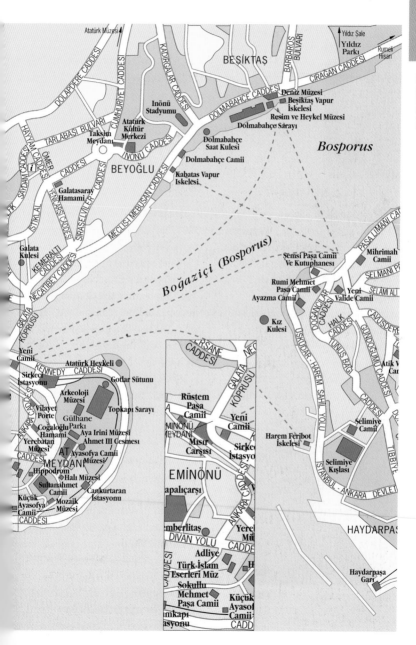

Atatürk Müzesi

Yıldız Şale
Yıldız Parkı
Rumeli Hisarı

BEŞİKTAŞ

DOLAPDERE CADDESI
KADIRGALAR CADDESI
BARBAROS BULVARI
CIRAĞAN CADDESI

TARLABAŞI BULVARI
CUMHURIYET CADDESI
DOLMABAHÇE CADDESI

İnönü Stadyumu

Deniz Müzesi
Beşiktaş Vapur İskelesi
Resim ve Heykel Müzesi
Dolmabahçe Sarayı

Atatürk Kültür Merkezi
Taksim Meydanı
İNÖNÜ CADDESI

Dolmabahçe Saat Kulesi

Bosporus

HAYYAM CADDESI
ÖMER CADDESI
CADDESI

BEYOĞLU

Dolmabahçe Camii

Galatasaray Hamamı

Kabataş Vapur İskelesi

İSTIKLAL
TEPEBAŞI CADDESI
SIRASELVILER CADDESI
MECLIS-I MEBUSAN CADDESI

Galata Kulesi

KEMERALTI CADDESI
NECATIBEY CADDESI

Boğaziçi (Bosporus)

Şemsi Paşa Camii Ve Kutuphanesı

Mihrimah Camii

PAŞA LIMANI CA

SELMANI P

Rumi Mehmet Paşa Camii
Ayazma Camii

Yeni Valide Camii

SELAMI ALTI

GALATA KÖPRÜSÜ

Kız Kulesi

ÜSKÜDAR-HAREM SAHIL YOLU
DOĞANCILAR CADDESI
HALK CADDESI
GÜNDOĞUMU CADDESI
ÇAVUSDERE
TUNUS BAĞI

Yeni Camii

TERSANE CADDESI
GALATA KÖPRÜSÜ
NEC

Atatürk Heykeli

Atik V
Car

Sirkeci İstasyonu
KENNEDY CADDESI

Gotlar Sütunu

Rüstem Paşa Camii

Yeni Camii

Arkeoloji Müzesi

Vilayet Porte
Gülhane Parkı
Topkapı Sarayı

ANKARA CADDESI

EMINÖNÜ MEYDANI

Mısır Çarşısı

Harem Feribot İskelesi

Selimiye Camii

Coğaloğlu Hamamı
Aya Irini Müzesi
Yerebatan Müzesi
Ahmet III Çeşmesi

Sirkeci İstasyo

İSTANBUL-ANKARA DEVLET

Selimiye Kışlası

TIBBIYE

AT MEYDANI
Ayasofya Camii Müzesi

DOĞA

CADDESI

Hippodrom
Halı Müzesi
Sultanahmet Camii
Küçük Ayasofya Camii
Mozaik Müzesi

Cankurtaran İstasyonu

kapalıçarşı

HAYDARPAŞ

CADDESI

mberlitaş
DIVAN YOLU

Yerel Mü
CADDE

Adliye
Türk-İslam Eserleri Müz
Sokullu Mehmet Paşa Camii

Küçük Ayasof Camii

Haydarpaşa Garı

ımkapı asyonu

CADD

Ayasofya Camii

Cathedral of Saint Sophia

There can be few places with such an overwhelming sense of history. On entering, the interior is magnificent and awesome. Here is the centre of what was Byzantine Constantinople, an extraordinary building, whose history is the very mirror of Byzantium itself.

Dedicated to Saint Sophia, the Divine Wisdom, by the Emperor Justinian in AD 537, the current building is the last of three churches on this site. The first two were both destroyed by fire. Architecturally the building is extremely complex. The vast shallow dome caused enormous structural stresses, which have made it vulnerable to earthquake damage throughout its history. To compensate, the massive flying buttresses were added. When the Crusaders sacked Constantinople in 1204 they stripped the interior of all movables. It then served as the Roman Catholic cathedral of the city throughout the Crusader occupation. The 15th century saw Constantinople in decay, and the cathedral too fell to ruin. The last Christian service was held here in 1453, the day before the Turks took the city.

When the conquering Sultan Mehmet II entered the city on that day, he rode straight to St Sophia and ordered it to be converted into a mosque with immediate effect. The following Friday the first Muslim prayers were held in it. Minarets, a *mihrab* and a *minbar* were added soon after, and the conversion was complete. Of the four minarets, the brick one was built first. The three stone ones at the other corners were added by Sinan (*see right*) in the 16th century.

The building was well maintained throughout the Ottoman period and successive sultans ordered restorations.

The dome of Ayasofya Camii was such an architectural marvel that people feared it would collapse

The mosaics were covered with whitewash, which helped a great deal to preserve them in the state we see today.

The mosque has been a museum since 1934. As you enter, look out for the immense doors sheathed in bronze, which date back to Justinian's time. The stonework in the nave interior is breathtaking, especially the colossal columns of purple porphyry and dark green verd antique marble. This verd antique is known to have been specially quarried for the cathedral from Thessaly. The porphyry, which must have come from Egypt, where the only quarries for this volcanic marble are to be found, is thought to have been taken from another, more ancient, building. The columns are topped with magnificent capitals carved in acanthus leaves. Throughout the church a colossal variety of rare and beautiful marble has been used.

A few mosaics have survived at the lower levels, notably the *Virgin Mary with the Christ Child on her Knees*, but the most magnificent are in the galleries, which are reached by a cobbled ramp that zigzags upwards. These galleries were used for the imperial family and other dignitaries. The most famous gallery mosaic, not to be missed, is the *Deesis*, with Christ in the centre, the Virgin Mary on one side, and an agonised John the Baptist on the other.

Scattered in the precincts outside are several domed imperial Ottoman tombs. *Ayasofya Camii, Sultanahmet. Open:*

The vast interior of Ayasofya Camii

Tue–Sun 9am–4.30pm. Closed: Mon. Admission charge. Entry is from the Ayasofya Meydanı side, which faces the Blue Mosque.

SINAN

Sinan is unquestionably the greatest Muslim architect. A near contemporary of Michelangelo, he is credited with 81 large mosques, 50 smaller mosques, 19 mausoleums, 32 palaces, 22 public baths, 2 bridges and 6 aqueducts – 84 of his buildings are still standing in Istanbul alone. He was born of Greek Christian parents in 1491 and later assigned to the Janissaries as a military engineer. He was nearly 50 when he completed his first mosque. He died at the age of 97.

Haliç (Golden Horn)

This inlet of the Bosporus is crossed by three bridges: the Galata, beside Eminönü Square; the Atatürk, which runs up and under the Aqueduct of Valens; and the Fatih Köprüsü (Haliç motorway bridge), in the north, running from the airport to the first Bosporus Bridge.

Kapalıçarşı (Covered Bazaar)

This 'landmark' is invisible, except from the air! You can only see it when you are inside (*see pp52–3*).

Stamboul

This is the Western way of referring to the original Constantinople, the area where Ayasofya, the Blue Mosque, the Topkapı and the Süleymaniye still stand.

Üsküdar

An important suburb of Istanbul, Üsküdar lies on the Asian side of the Bosporus, directly opposite the mouth of the Golden Horn. Ferries run from the Galata Bridge every 15 minutes to reach Üsküdar (*see pp38–9*).

CHURCHES
Aya Irini (St Irene)

This vast and peaceful basilica is second in size only to Ayasofya. It lies in a corner of the outermost fourth court of the palace and is a haven of tranquillity. Its name, suitably, means divine peace. The current building dates from the 6th century. The Turks used it as an arsenal for the Janissaries, the military élite

guard of the sultan, who were barracked in this court. It is used for exhibitions and concerts, especially during the Istanbul Festival. The acoustics are superb.

Aya Irini Müzesi, close to the Topkapı Palace entrance. Open to the public only for special events.

Ayasofya (St Sophia)

See pp32–3.

Bulgar Kilisesi
(St Stephen of the Bulgars)

This remarkable church is made entirely of cast iron. It was prefabricated in Vienna in 1871, then shipped down the Danube and across the Black Sea to be assembled here. The tiny Bulgarian community still worship here regularly.

Its location on the western side of the Golden Horn enhances its attractive appearance. A guardian lives in a hut within its railed garden and will open the church for a small consideration.

Mürsel Paşa Caddesi, Fener. Open: always, when the guardian is in attendance. Admission free, but leave a small tip.

Imrahor Camii
(St John the Baptist of Studius)

This vast ruined hulk is the oldest surviving Christian monument in the city, completed in AD 463. Set in a walled courtyard, it is still very impressive. The church was once the centre of a monastic community housing 1,000 monks.

Imam Asir Sokak, near Yedikule. Visit the Directorate at Ayasofya Museum for entry information.

Kariye Camii (St Saviour's in Chora)

After Ayasofya this is the most important Byzantine church in the city, now turned into a small museum to display its own mosaic murals and frescoes, which are considered the finest examples of Byzantine art in the world. The church is set in a charming courtyard; it is a quiet spot with just a handful of stalls selling up-market souvenirs.

The name 'in Chora' means 'in the country', for the church was originally outside the city walls. The small scale of the church makes the mosaics here seem very accessible, almost intimate. They date from the early 14th century and, thanks to restoration, remain in very good condition.

The mosaics relate the life story of the Virgin Mary and the life of Christ from infant to adult in unusual detail. Mary is rebuked in one scene by Joseph when he returns from a journey to find her pregnant. In the next scene he is reassured by a dream that she is telling the truth about the conception of her baby.

Other striking scenes depict Christ's temptation by the devil and Christ's miracles, notably walking on water, the feeding of the 5,000, and turning the water into wine. There is also a startling resurrection scene with Christ pulling Adam and Eve from their tombs.

Near the Edirnekapı (Edirne Gate).
Open: Wed–Mon 9am–5pm.
Closed: Tue. Admission charge.

Küçük Ayasofya (Saints Sergius and Bacchus)

Converted to a mosque in the early 16th century and still in use today, this former church is one of the most beautiful old Byzantine churches surviving in the city. The old quarter in

arrowing of Hell, with Christ pulling Adam and Eve from their tombs, Kariye Camii

The Byzantine Empire

In a move that symbolised the decline of Rome and the separation of the eastern and western halves of the Roman Empire, the Emperor Constantine founded a new capital at Constantinople in AD 330. While the western empire collapsed in AD 476, the eastern half (called Byzantine after Byzantium, the Greek name for the earlier town on the site) survived until 1453, when the Ottoman Turks finally extinguished it.

The Byzantine Empire was left with two major legacies: the preservation of Greek culture and the creation of Orthodox Christianity as a state religion, with Byzantine emperors playing the roles of Caesar and Pope combined. These emperors, notably Justinian, provided lavish patronage for artists and architects, resulting in the development of the classic Byzantine domed basilica, of which the 6th-century Ayasofya is the most outstanding example (*see pp32–3*). All Byzantine churches in Constantinople were built of brick, with little exterior decoration. Inside, by contrast, they

The Anastasis fresco in the Kariye Camii, Istanbul

Christ Pantocrator mosaic, Kariye Camii, Istanbul

were ablaze with colour from mosaics, often depicting biblical story cycles. In Ayasofya, only fragments of these mosaics are visible, but those in the Church of St Saviour in Chora (now the Kariye Museum, *see p35*) are recognised as the most stunning and complete example of Byzantine mosaic art. Veneration of icons (images of Christ, the Virgin and the saints) also began in the Byzantine era, and an elaborately stylised iconography developed to work out which items from the Bible should be represented where in the church. All pictorial decorations were, alas, destroyed by the zealous iconoclasts (image- or icon-breakers), whose hegemony lasted from AD 711 until 843, which is why the extant mosaics in Istanbul today all date from the mid-9th century onwards.

The Byzantine style of art and architecture spread outwards to neighbouring regions, so we can still see domed churches of remarkable similarity across Italy, Greece and the Balkans, all of which are frequently decorated with mosaics and icons.

which the mosque stands has wooden houses with carved overhanging balconies. The church was built by Justinian in AD 527 before Ayasofya, which it is said to resemble.

Inside, climb the stairs to the gallery to view the church decorations. Peering out through the windows at the overgrown graveyard, the setting has an almost rural feel.

Küçük Ayasofya Caddesi, Sultanahmet. Open: At all times, like all working mosques. Free admission.

MOSQUES

All these working mosques are open daily and can be visited except during the five periods of prayer. There are no entry fees, but a small tip (*baksheesh*) is usually expected by the shoe attendant.

Ayasofya Camii

See pp32–3.

Beyazit Camii

The Beyazıt (built 1501) is the earliest imperial mosque extant in the city. The mosque has a charming courtyard with fine porphyry, verd antique marble and granite columns and insets. Steps from the courtyard lead to the open yard under the famous plane tree, where students gather for tea.

On the hill between Istanbul University and the Covered Bazaar.

Eyüp Sultan Camii

See pp54–5.

Fatih Camii

This mosque complex is the biggest and most elaborate in Istanbul and indeed in the entire Ottoman Empire. Built by Mehmet the Conqueror in 1463, the Turkish name means 'conquest'. Size is the distinguishing feature of the Fatih rather than architectural merit. Of the associated buildings, the hospice and hospital deserve a visit for their beautiful courtyards.

Tophane Sokağı, Fatih. On one of the highest hills of Stamboul, north of the Süleymaniye Camii.

Mihrimah Sultan Camii (Edirne Kapi)

This exquisite mosque is one of Sinan's masterpieces (*see p33*), built for the Princess Mihrimah, Süleyman the Magnificent's favourite daughter.

Raised up on a platform just inside the Edirne Gate.

Rüstem Paşa Camii

Built in 1561, this is one of Sinan's (*see p33*) finest small mosques. It is famous above all for the superb Iznik tiles that

Istanbul's Blue Mosque

virtually cover the walls. The mosque is entered by climbing internal steps beside some vaulted shops.

Hidden in a side street up the hill from Eminönü Square.

Şemsi Paşa Camii

This little gem, built by Sinan of white stone in 1580, stands right on the edge of the water, at the confluence of the Bosporus and the Sea of Marmara, on the Asian side.

Sahil Yolu, Üsküdar.

Sokullu Mehmet Paşa Camii

This is considered the most beautiful of the smaller mosques of the city, built by Sinan (*see p33*) in 1571. Sokullu Mehmet was Grand Vizier (chief adviser) to Süleyman the Magnificent and his son Selim II. The small interior is exquisitely decorated with Iznik tiles.

Above the door lintel is a small square fragment of the black Kaaba stone, the sacred stone of Mecca that was given to Adam.

Şehit Mehmet Paşa Sokak 20–24, Sultanahmet.

Süleymaniye Camii

This is regarded as the most beautiful imperial mosque of the city. It is a masterpiece of the great Ottoman architect, Sinan, and is a fitting testimony to its founder Süleyman the Magnificent, whose tomb and that of his wife Roxelana (*see right*) lie within the complex. The colossal dark grey stone mosque was finished in 1557 and took seven years in the building. The mausoleum is the largest and grandest Sinan ever built. Sinan's own *türbe* lies in a modest corner just beyond the caravanserai. The other buildings here are the theological schools, hospital, hamam and kitchens.

Şifahane Sokak, Süleymaniye. East up the hill from Eminönü Square.

Sultanahmet Camii (Blue Mosque)

Completed in 1616, the Blue Mosque dominates the skyline of Istanbul with its six tall minarets, vying with the Süleymaniye for the title of supreme imperial mosque of Istanbul. During the centuries that the sultans resided at the Topkapı Palace, an imperial procession would take place each Friday down to this mosque to attend the noonday prayers. The splendid ablution fountain in the centre of the monumental courtyard is where the ritual washing before prayer still takes place.

The interior is unusually light, with 260 windows. The predominant colour in the painted arabesques and the tiles is blue, giving the mosque its popular name. The Iznik tiles that cover the

ROXELANA

Roxelana 'The Russian' was Süleyman the Magnificent's favourite wife. In her ambitions for her own son, Selim the Sot, she persuaded Süleyman to murder his elder son Mustafa, so that Selim could succeed to the throne. The drunken Selim's rule is generally reckoned as the beginning of the end for the Ottoman Empire.

lower part of the walls are of the highest quality, in subtle blues and greens with elaborate floral designs of lilies, tulips and roses. The other striking internal features are the four marble columns supporting the dome, impressively huge with 5m (16½ft) diameters.

Mimar Mehmet Ağa Caddesi, Sultanahmet.

Yeni Camii (New Mosque)

Of no special architectural merit, this mosque, built in 1597, is well known because of its prominent location.

Eminönü Square, beside the Galata Bridge and the Egyptian Spice Market.

MUSEUMS
Arkeoloji Müzesi (Archaeological Museum)

The Archaeological Museum is a vast and fascinating place, boasting one of the richest collections of Greco-Roman statues and antiquities in the world, along with a remarkable collection of sarcophagi dating from the 4th century BC, which was discovered by a Turkish archaeologist at the royal necropolis of Sidon, Lebanon. One is known as the Alexander Sarcophagus because of the battle scenes depicted on its sides. The halls on the ground floor contain Greek and Roman statues.

The Ancient Orient Museum, part of the Archaeological Museum, is a fascinating and digestible display of ancient Egyptian, Babylonian and Hittite artefacts. Most memorable are the Hittite statues, from the colossal lions flanking the entrance to the sphinxes and larger-than-life storm gods inside. Among the most striking exhibits are the wall lions dating from Nebuchadnezzar's Babylon (5th century BC), made from colourful brick tiles, predominantly yellows and blues.

The Çinili Köşk (Tile Kiosk) constitutes the third element of the museum. A beautiful pavilion, built in 1472 as part of Topkapı Palace (*see pp46–7*), the rooms themselves are tiled, as well as displaying rare and exquisite examples in display cases.

The museum lies within the Topkapı Palace walls, signposted from the Fourth Court. Open: Tue–Sun 9am–5pm. Closed: Mon.

Hali Müzesi (Turkish Carpets Museum)

This museum, housed in a small royal pavilion, has a remarkable collection of carpets ranging from the 15th to the 19th centuries.

Kabasakal Caddesi, Sultanahmet (beside the Blue Mosque at the northeast corner). Open: Tue–Sat 9.30am–5pm. Closed: Sun & Mon. Admission charge.

Statues at the Archaeological Museum in Istanbul

Kariye Müzesi (Kariye Museum)

See p35.

Mozaik Müzesi (Mosaic Museum)

These are the *in situ* displays of mosaic pavements from the Great Palace of Byzantium, discovered in 1935. The mosaics are thought to date back to AD 500 and show animated scenes of Byzantine life.

Kabasakal Caddesi, Sultanahmet (behind the restored Ottoman St market by the Blue Mosque).

Open: Tue, Wed, Fri–Sun, 1 Oct–28 Feb 9.30am–4pm; 1 Mar–30 Sept 9.30am–5pm. Closed: Mon & Thur.

Sadberk Hanim Muzesi (Sadberk Hanim Museum)

Located in a handsome *yalı* (summerhouse) on the upper Bosporus shore between Büyükdere and Sarıyer, this museum houses a unique collection of Turkish works of art, and was founded by the wife of one of Turkey's leading businessmen.

Piyasa Caddesi, Büyükdere (a short walk north from Büyükdere landing stage).

Open: Thur–Tue 10am–5pm. Admission charge.

Topkapi Sarahi Müzesi (Topkapi Palace Museum)

See pp46–7.

Türk-Islam Eserleri Müzesi (Museum of Turkish and Islamic Art)

A splendid 19th-century palace, this is the grandest private residence ever built in the Ottoman Empire. Its attractive gallery overlooks the Hippodrome and the Blue Mosque and now serves as a teahouse.

The building was the home of Ibrahim Pasha, Grand Vizier to Süleyman the Magnificent, who was married to Süleyman's sister, but Süleyman's favourite wife Roxelana (*see p39*) convinced Süleyman that Ibrahim was becoming a threat to his own authority and Süleyman dutifully arranged for his slaves to murder Ibrahim.

The interior courtyard of marble paving with a garden has been beautifully restored. The exhibits are extremely well displayed and include miniatures, manuscripts and calligraphy, ceramics and glass, woodwork and carpets. There is also an intriguing display of the tent-life of the nomadic Yürük, forebears of the Turks.

Binbirdirek (opposite the Blue Mosque beside the Hippodrome).

Open: Tue–Sun 9.30am–4.30pm. Closed: Mon. Admission charge.

Yerebatan Sarayı Müzesi (Underground Museum)

This vast underground cistern should not be missed. Now fully restored, it was originally built in AD 532 by Justinian to store water for the emperor's Great Palace.

The entrance is only identifiable from the queue of people buying tickets, as nothing exists at ground level. There follows a slippery descent into the still water-filled cistern, with its total of 336 columns, by far the largest Roman cistern in the city. Opera music sets the atmosphere, and the only other sound is dripping water. The wooden walkways over the water can be slippery, so keep a firm hold of excited children or elderly companions. Notice the upside-down and sideways huge Medusa heads at the far end, clearly pilfered from an earlier temple, an unexpected sight in this unforgettable place.

The cistern was rediscovered in the 16th century, when a local architect heard that the houses in the neighbourhood obtained their water by lowering buckets from their basements, sometimes catching fish in the process.

Yerebatan Caddesi, Sultanahmet (a short walk across the street from Ayasofya Meydanı).
Open: daily 9am–5pm.
Admission charge.

PALACES
Aynalikavak Kasri
(Palace of the Mirroring Poplars)

This attractive late-Ottoman palace has been restored with décor dating from the 19th century. It is renowned for its numerous windows, many of them stained glass. It is rarely visited because it lies off the tourist track on the eastern side of the Golden Horn.

Kasımpaşa-Hasköy Yolu, Hasköy (500m/ 550yds from the Hasköy landing stage on the Golden Horn). Open: Tue, Wed & Fri–Sun 9.30am–4pm. Admission charge.

Beylerbeyi Sarayı
(Beylerbeyi Palace)

The grandest palace ever built on the Asian side of Istanbul was intended as a summer palace for the later Ottoman sultans and a guesthouse for visiting royalty. Its interior is as lavish as that of the Dolmabahçe (*see p43*). The architects of these two palaces were brothers. It is best reached by taking a ferry to Üsküdar, from where it is a five-minute taxi ride.

Abdullah Ağa Caddesi, Beylerbeyi (immediately north of the first Bosporus Bridge, on the Asian side). Open: Tue, Wed & Fri–Sun, 1 Oct–28 Feb 9.30am–4pm; 1 Mar–30 Sept 9.30am–5pm. Admission charge.

Blachernae Sarayı

Little survives of the Byzantine palace Blachernae Sarayı, which is tucked in a poor quarter of the city just inside the walls. Now landscaped with a children's playground, the best view of it is from the terrace of the adjacent Ivaz Efendi Mosque.

Toklu Dede Sokak, Ayvansaray (beside the Ivaz Efendi Mosque). Open: always. Free admission.

Bucoleon Sarayı

All along the Sea of Marmara from Küçük Ayasofya Mosque to the Kalyon Hotel is a stretch of well-preserved Byzantine sea wall built by Constantine the Great. Set in these walls is a marble-sided arched gateway known as Çatladı Kapı, the Imperial Marine

The Dolmabahçe Palace

Dolmabahçe Sarayı (Dolmabahçe Palace)

The most fabulously lavish palace in Turkey, with a breathtaking 600m (650yd) frontage on to the Bosporus, this white marble rococo-style palace was commissioned by Sultan Abdul Mejid in 1834 after he had become depressed by living in the Topkapı Palace and desired a change. The architect was a Turkish Armenian, Garabet Balyan. The sultans of the later years of the Ottoman Empire all moved here, leaving the Topkapı abandoned.

Once into the gardens, where there is a pleasant café and souvenir shop, all is peaceful away from the traffic noise. Head for the palace itself, where conducted tours head off round the interior every 15 minutes and last for nearly an hour.

The official rooms are still sometimes used for special functions, and the elaborately ornate decoration is reminiscent of French palaces such as Versailles. The bird pavilion still houses species from all over the world.

Dolmabahçe Caddesi, Beşiktaş (500m/ 550yds from the Kabataş landing stage on the European side of the Bosporus). Open: Tue, Wed & Fri–Sun 9am–4pm. Admission charge (extra to use cameras or video cameras). The palace has a daily quota of 1,500 visitors and closes after this is reached.

Küçüksu Kasrı (Little Water Palace)

Sometimes called Göksu Palace, this exquisite 19th-century rococo palace

Gate, which was the entrance to the Bucoleon Palace. Three marble-framed windows of the palace can be seen a little further west. This is all that now remains of Constantine's magnificent Great Palace of Byzantium, built when he first founded his new capital in AD 330. It was sacked by the Crusaders in 1204, and by the time of the Turkish conquest in 1453, the palace was in ruins.
Bucoleon Caddesi, Kennedy Caddesi, Sultanahmet. Open: always. Free admission.

Çirağan Sarayı (Çirağan Kempinski Hotel)

Gutted by fire in 1910, this palace stood as a ruined shell for decades, until it was renovated to become arguably the most luxurious hotel in Istanbul.
Çirağan Kempinski Oteli, Çirağan Caddesi, Beşiktaş (on the Bosporus at the foot of the Yıldız Park). The bars and restaurants are open to non-residents.

stands on the Asian Bosporus shore between the streams known as the Sweet Waters of Asia. The Ottoman sultans used it for holidaying, and the meadows around are still popular for family picnics at weekends.

Küçüksu Caddesi, Göksu (just south of the new Bosporus Bridge, on the Asian side, a short walk from Küçüksu landing stage). Open: Tue, Wed & Fri–Sun. Admission charge.

Tekfur Sarayı
(Palace of the Porphyrogenitus)

An unexpectedly magnificent façade of this Byzantine residence of the 13th century survives, tucked just inside the walls. Built of red brick and white marble, it still stands three storeys high.

Şişehane Caddesi, Avcı bey (west from Eğrikapı, inside the walls). Open: always. Admission free, but the resident guardian family expects a tip.

Yildiz Sarayı (Yildiz Palace)

Set at the top of the magnificent Yıldız Park, Yildiz is a late 19th-century palace that included a complex of pavilions and a mosque. Because of restoration work only one pavilion, the Şale, is open to the public at present.

Yıldız Caddesi, Yıldız (on the hill beyond Beyoğlu next to the Yıldız University). Open: Tue, Wed & Fri–Sun 9am–5pm. Admission charge.

PARKS AND CITY WALLS

Istanbul is a city deceptively rich in parks and open spaces. All the parks

mentioned are open to the public free of charge from 8am till dusk.

Haliç (Golden Horn)

The whole western shoreline of the Golden Horn has been landscaped, making peaceful strolling while gazing at the impressive skyline of the old city (*see pp54–5*). North of the new Galata Bridge you can see segments of the famous old Galata Bridge with its floating restaurants, which had to be dismantled in May 1992 after a gas explosion in one of the restaurants blew a hole in the middle of the bridge

Gülhane Parkı (Gülhane Park)

Once part of the Topkapı Palace, this is now a fine public park on the hillside below the palace. From the fountain outside the Topkapı walls, the main entrance to the park is reached by following the cobbled street that leads down Soğukçeşme Sokak past the old Ottoman houses that are now hotels. The southern end of the park is taken up by Istanbul Zoo. The zoo's aquarium is housed in a Roman cistern.

Karaca Ahmet Mezarlik
(Karaca Ahmed Cemetery)

A lovely and unusual place for a stroll, this enormous graveyard in Üsküdar is the largest and oldest Muslim cemetery in Turkey. Take a ferry to Üsküdar, then a taxi up the hill to the Karaca Ahmet Camii, beside which is the main entrance to the cemetery.

Gündoğümü Caddesi, Üsküdar.

Yildiz Parkı

A fabulously landscaped Ottoman park covering a hillside overlooking the Bosporus, this is a tranquil place to stroll and sip tea in one of the beautifully restored kiosks or conservatories with dramatic Bosporus views. It is easily the loveliest park in Istanbul.
Yıldız Caddesi, Yıldız.

The city walls

The mighty land walls which protected the city of Byzantium from its enemies for over 1,000 years still stand for most of their 6.5km (4-mile) length. To walk along them these days is quite ambitious and should only be attempted when the weather has been dry for several consecutive days. In parts you can stroll along the ramparts, and where this is not possible, you have to judge whether it is more convenient to walk inside or outside the walls.

The land walls were originally built under Emperor Theodosius II in the 5th century. There were 96 defence towers.

The impregnability of these Byzantine land walls altered the course of history, when Attila the Hun, Scourge of God, thwarted by the power of the walls, directed his wrath instead on the western Roman Empire.

Today, most people drive round the outside of the walls to get a feel of their scope, but the point at which you should certainly stop is **Yedikule**, the Castle of the Seven Towers, which stands near the Sea of Marmara, approached from Kennedy Caddesi. Part of the tower was used as a prison, part as storage for the state treasure. It was also the main place of execution, and instruments of torture used by the Ottomans are on display here. On the outer wall is the so-called Golden Gate, originally a Roman triumphal arch dated AD 390. Its doors were originally covered in gold plate, but were later walled up for defence and never reopened.
Yedikule Müzesi, Kapı Yol, Yedikule.
Open: Tue–Sun 10am–4pm.
Closed: Mon. Admission charge.

Istanbul

A restored section of Istanbul's city walls

Topkapı Sarayı

Topkapı Palace

This palace is today an incomparable museum of Ottoman wealth and splendour, beautifully laid out in the rooms. With one of the most fabulous settings of any palace anywhere, the Topkapı stands on the promontory jutting out between the Bosporus and the Golden Horn, the first hill of the Seven Hills of Istanbul.

The palace has four courtyards, and the entrance to the first one is marked by the fabulous free-standing rococo street fountain of Ahmet III with its own overhanging roof. Built in 1728, it is the most beautiful and elaborate Ottoman fountain in the city, as befits its location. The ticket office lies within the first court, the Court of the Janissaries, where the sultan's élite military corps of slave soldiers was stationed. In the extreme southeast corner stands the impressive basilica of Aya Irini. During confidential meetings with officials and dignitaries, the sultan would instruct that the fountains be turned on so that no one could overhear their discussions.

The entrance to the third court is flanked by two magnificent octagonal towers. The main walkway through is lined with cypress trees, two of which have curiously interbred with a fig and a plane tree to form hybrids. Byzantine cisterns run under this walkway, and traces of the red brickwork can still be seen under the paving. The harem lies over to the far western end of the courtyard and the separate ticket kiosk stands outside it.

Little is really known for sure about life in the harem. Much is gossip and hearsay. The women were guarded by black eunuchs, and even the chief physician was only allowed to inspect his patients' hands. The lucky woman in favour on any particular night would be summoned to the imperial bedchamber, told to kiss the imperial coverlet at the foot end, then wriggle her way under it to encounter the sultan. No Turkish woman is thought ever to have had this honour, only thousands of Caucasians, Georgians and Armenians, and a handful of Western Europeans. Murat III (1574–95) had 1,200 harem women and fathered 103 children by them.

Problems inevitably arose in such circumstances about how to decide the succession, and the usual Ottoman solution was wholesale slaughter of the other contenders by the eldest. When this custom was thought to be getting out of hand, a new method was introduced of locking up the younger brothers in the royal prison within the Topkapı, known as the Kafes. One of the busiest halls in the palace is the Pavilion of the Holy Mantle, containing Muslim holy relics captured during Selim the Grim's campaign in Egypt in the 16th century. In addition to rare examples of the Koran, these include a lock of Mohammed's beard hair and a cast of the footprint he left as he ascended into heaven.

Within the palace, the kitchens occupy the biggest single building. There were ten different ones, each catering for a different hierarchy. Today they house a priceless ceramics collection.

For most people the highlight of the museum is the Treasury, where the accumulated jewels and treasure of the Ottoman sultans are displayed. Here you can see some of the biggest emeralds and diamonds in the world, and the famous Topkapı dagger. It tends to be the most crowded part of the museum.

Beyond in the furthermost court are the ornate kiosks and terraces with fabulous views, where the restaurant and café make lingering even more of a pleasure.

Sultanahmet. Tel: 512 0480. Open: Wed–Mon 9am–5pm. Admission charge. There is an additional charge for a tour of the harem, queued for and bought separately inside the palace, and the Treasury. Tours of the harem leave every 30 minutes, 9.30am–3.30pm.

Topkapı Palace, mosaics in the kiosks

The Turkish bath

There are said to be about 100 old Ottoman baths, called *hamam* in Istanbul, of which about 80 are still in use. There is little doubt that their popularity will continue, as the fuel shortage makes a weekly visit to the *hamam* an attractive proposition. The degree of all-over cleanliness it produces is way beyond what most of us ever achieve through our daily baths and showers. As a British clergyman wrote in the 1930s during his stay here: 'They hold impurity of the body in greater detestation than impurity of the mind, ablution being so essential that without it prayer will be of no value in the eyes of God.'

Ottoman marriage contracts stipulated that a husband had to give his wife bath-money. If he failed to do so it was grounds for divorce.

Mixed bathing is not permitted except in some of the larger hotels, and the penalty for a man entering

Coy men of the Çemberlitas Baths

Massage in action at the Galatasaray Baths

the women's *hamam* used to be death. The women's baths are delightfully relaxing places, with fat homely masseuses in black briefs with colossal swinging bosoms, often smoking cigarettes in between customers. Nakedness is the norm among foreigners in a women's *hamam*. Since you are probably only going to do it once, have everything on offer – the rub with the rough glove to shed years of grime from your front and especially your back, the soaping, the face massage and even the foot massage. Even with all

the extras the whole experience is still remarkably good value. Each person has a locker for their valuables. The men's baths, by contrast, sound a lot less fun, with towels wrapped firmly round waists.

The baths recommended for foreigners are the Çağaloğlu (Yerebatan Caddesi), the Çemberlıtas (Vezirhan Caddesi 8) in Sultanahmet, and the Galatasaray in Turnacibasi Caddesi, Beyoğlu. Some of the big five-star hotels also have small Turkish baths, but they lack the authentic atmosphere.

ISTANBUL ENVIRONS
Adalar (Princes' Islands)

These nine islands, of which only four are inhabited, are an hour's ferry ride south from Istanbul, making popular weekend retreats. No cars are allowed, and the only means of transport for visitors and inhabitants alike is horse and carriage.

Çanakkale Boğazıçı (The Dardanelles)

This is the ancient Hellespont, the straits that separate Europe from Asia. Legend has it that Leander swam across them each night to visit his lover Hero, until drowned in a storm. The endless coming and going of boats of all shapes and sizes can be watched from one of Çanakkale's seafront cafés.

Bursa

At four hours' drive from Istanbul, this city is just feasible as a day trip and many tour companies offer it. Famed as a spa town for many centuries, it is also visited for its splendid mosques, the best of which is Yeşil Camii (Green Mosque), built between 1413 and 1421 for Sultan Mehmed I. The *türbe* of the sultan lies in the grounds and is decorated with impressive tiles.

There are other impressive, though less elaborate, tombs in the grounds of Muradiye Camii. These honour notable Ottoman dignitaries who worked at the court in Bursa during its era as capital of the empire. Ulu Camii (Great Mosque) lies at the heart of Bursa's bazaar district, surrounded by a maze of narrow streets filled with stalls and shops.

Although most large Bursa hotels have modern spa facilities, the district of Çekirge hosts a selection of historic complexes. The oldest and most interesting is the Baths of Eskikaplıca, dating from the 14th century.

Edirne (Adrianople)

The only reason most people visit Edirne is to see the Selimiye Mosque, the building which Sinan himself always maintained was the culmination of his career. Built when he was 85 years old, Sinan brought together all his experience and research in Ottoman architecture to achieve this vast construction, its four minarets each over 70m (230ft) tall.

Mimar Sinan Caddesi (town centre). A working mosque. Open: daily, except at prayer times.

Gülets moored along the quayside at Marmaris

Istanbul environs

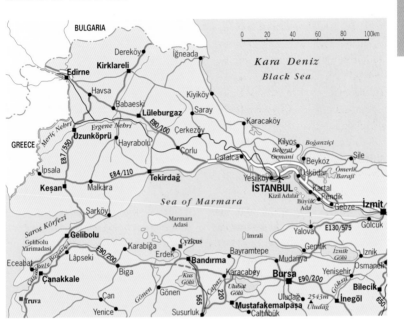

Gelibolu (Gallipoli)

This peninsula, where half a million soldiers lost their lives in World War I, is now a national park, containing various war memorials. It was here in 1915 that the Allies mounted a disastrous expedition against the Turks who had joined forces with the Germans.

FERRIES

To save road distances there are several car ferries across the Sea of Marmara. The major ones are Eceabat–Çanakkale, Gelibolu–Lapseki and Pendik–Yalova. They all take about 30 minutes, are cheap, and run throughout the day and evening.

ULUDAĞ

Turkey's premier winter ski resort, Uludağ is one hour's drive from Bursa, or 30 minutes in the cable car (*teleferik*) which runs several times a day, summer and winter.

Iznik (Nicaea)

Tiles were produced here from the 16th century onwards, but the town today is visited mainly for its lakeside fish restaurants. Its Byzantine walls are well preserved.

Marmara Denizi (Sea of Marmara)

Ringed by green rolling hills, the Sea of Marmara boasts many beaches and resorts, the major ones of which are Mudanya, Gemlik and Yalova, all on the Asian or southern shore.

Walk: Around the Covered Bazaar, Istanbul

The Bazaar, the largest in the world, has around 4,000 shops in total, employing some 30,000 people. Half a million people shop here every day. There are a dozen restaurants, several banks, numerous ATMs, teahouses and sandwich stalls, and it even has its own post office and police station. The best point of entry is the Nuru Osmaniye Gate. The Bazaar is open Mon–Sat 8.30am–7pm.

First impressions

Once inside, the first-time visitor will be struck by how clean and cheerful the Bazaar is, with high airy ceilings and lovely tilework on many walls and pillars. The sheer quantity of goods is overwhelming. On sale here are carpets, alabaster, antiques, ceramics, copper, brass, gold and silver, leather, suede, clothes, bags, shoes, backgammon sets, hubble-bubble pipes, meerschaum pipes, hats, fezzes, woolly socks and gloves knitted by the nomads of eastern Turkey – the list is endless.

Route planning as such never works, as the visitor invariably gets lured off down a tempting side street. There are two lines of approach. You can either just stick to the main streets, making a short sortie to the Iç Bedesten in the centre, or go round the edge, visiting all the hans (small workshops) where you can see many items being made.

Iç Bedesten

One place not to be missed is the Iç Bedesten right in the middle, one of the few buildings that survives from the

Tempting displays line the side streets

15th century, and where antiques, copper, gold and silver jewellery are sold in an area separated from the rest of the Bazaar by four gateways.

Orientation and merchandise

Throughout the Bazaar the trades are all grouped together, as is the oriental custom. The persistent touting is worst in the main streets, but if you go deeper into quieter side streets it stops. Money can be changed almost everywhere.

To watch silver items being made, or get something made or repaired, visit the Kalcılar Han in the northeast corner. The nearby Zincirli Han is also very attractive. For gold and jewels, many

shops are concentrated in Kuyumcular Caddesi, between Sandal Bedesteni and Iç Bedesten. The carpet merchants are around the Iç Bedesten. What is still called the Fesciler Caddesi (Street of the Fezmakers) now sells denim.

For books, new or second-hand, go to the Sahaflar Çarşısı. Lying, strictly speaking, just outside the Bazaar, it is always crowded with students.

Walk: Around the Covered Bazaar, Istanbul

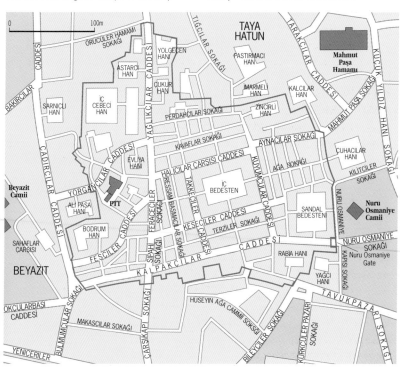

Walk: From Pierre Loti's Café at sunset, Istanbul

This must be one of the most relaxing walks in Istanbul. It is all downhill or on the flat, and you are almost always away from the traffic – unusual for this city.

Allow 3 hours for the full walk, incorporating all the sights en route. But even only an hour would be enough to give you a feel for the magnificent Haliç (Golden Horn) and the Istanbul skyline.

Begin by taking a taxi to Pierre Loti's Café in the northern district of Eyüp, a journey of about 20 minutes from the Blue Mosque area. Ideally, aim to arrive about two hours before sunset. The taxi bumps up the winding backstreets to deposit you at the back of the café. Perched on the edge of a steep drop, it overlooks the northern end of the Golden Horn and below it sprawls the large, picturesque graveyard of Eyüp, the holiest burial ground in Istanbul.

1 Pierre Loti's Café

The café, named after the French novelist who used to frequent it in the late 1800s, does not offer food but is a wonderful place for tea before the walk, with dramatic views from the terraces. *To begin, follow the wide stone path that leads off down the hillside through the graveyard, admiring the elaborate tombstones of wealthy Ottomans along*

the way. A leisurely descent takes about 15 minutes to the bottom.

Where the path meets the road, turn left then first right to reach the entrance of the Eyüp Sultan Camii and Türbesi.

2 Eyüp Sultan Camii (mosque) and Türbesi (tomb)

This is the third-holiest shrine in the Muslim world after Mecca and Jerusalem. Eyüp himself, standard-bearer and friend of the Prophet Muhammad, was said to have been killed here during the first Arab siege of Constantinople in AD 674. Except for the mosque (rebuilt in 1798), the current complex of buildings dates from 1458. The *imaret*, or soup kitchen, still serves some 500 local poor people at 11am each morning.

Entering the attractive courtyard through the two main gateways, Eyüp's tomb lies to the right. Leave your shoes outside, and step inside on to the carpets to admire the superb Iznik tiles covering the walls.

Leave the courtyard by the opposite gateway and turn left through the old market street of Eyüp, where you may see mysterious twigs in bunches for sale. These are used as toothbrushes by the poor.

Continue in a straight line across the main road to reach the shore near the Eyüp Vapur Iskelesi .

3 Haliç (Golden Horn)

This Stamboul shoreline is now parkland, and it is a delight to stroll along the water's edge. You can complete the full 3.5km (2 miles), looking at mosques and churches along the way, or break off at any time.

Walking under the motorway bridge, you soon come to the edge of the Byzantine land walls. A half-hour detour inland here takes the visitor to the ruined Blachernae Sarayı and the Tekfur Sarayı (see p42 & p44). Fragments of the Byzantine sea walls run all along the Golden Horn to the Atatürk bridge.

Returning to the Golden Horn, the first mosque after about 500m (550yds) is Atik Mustafa Paşa, a former 9th-century Byzantine church. Further on is St Stephen of the Bulgars (see p34).

4 Atatürk bridge

The walk ends at Atatürk bridge.

Walk: From Pierre Loti's Café at sunset, Istanbul

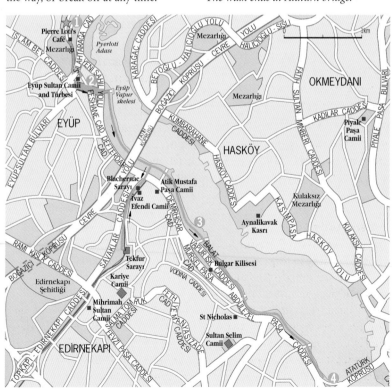

By boat: The Bosporus

One of the most historic waterways of the world, this extraordinary winding strait that links the Black Sea to the Mediterranean is 32km (20 miles) long, with a width that fluctuates from 500m to 3km (550yds to 2 miles). Most organised cruises that run along it take half a day, but if you have time, turn it into a full day by getting off at the northernmost point of Anadolu Kavağı to have lunch, then hiring a taxi to take you back along the Asian shore.

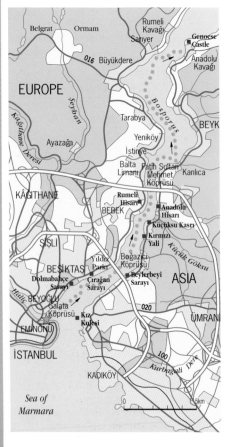

The public steamers that plough up and down the Bosporus from the embarkation point at Eminönü by the Galata Köprüsü (Galata bridge), run frequently and are the equivalent of the local bus service. They have to be queued for in crowded halls and the boats themselves are rather shabby and squalid, with limited on-deck seating. If you sit inside you do not get very good views, so it is preferable in the tourist season (mid-April to mid-October) to take the special tour boats, which are much more luxurious and cruise much closer to the main sights.

The tour boats leave twice daily (morning and afternoon) from Eminonu, or the Bosporus Ferry Boat landing pier below the Topkapı, about 400m (440yds) from the Galata bridge.

The first leg

When the boat sets off, it is best to focus initially on the views backwards towards the Topkapı and the mosque skyline. Then, after gliding past the **Dolmabahçe Sarayı** (*see p43*), the boat makes its first stop at **Beşiktaş**.

Beşiktaş to Kanlica

Just beyond **Beşiktaş** is the vast restored waterfront palace, **Çırağan Sarayı**, which is now the Çırağan-Kempinksi Hotel (*see p43*).

The eye is drawn next by the colossal 1973 **Boğazıçı Köprüsü** (Bosporus bridge), and tucked just beyond it on the Asian side is the **Beylerbeyi Sarayı** (palace). When the 1987 Fatih Sultan **Mehmet Koprüsü**, the third-longest suspension bridge in the world, looms into view, you can spot, again on the Asian side, the splendid **Kırmızı Yali**, the Red Mansion, the best-preserved seaside mansion on the Bosporus, and about 500m (550yds) further north towards the bridge, the little white palace of **Küçüksu**.

Immediately beyond Küçüksu, just before the bridge, are two castles opposite each other, **Rumeli Hisarı** on the European side and **Anadolu Hisarı** on the Asian side. This is the narrowest point of the Bosporus, at a mere 500m (550yds), and the same spot where the Persian king Darius chose to build his bridge of boats to transport his army across.

The boat stops at Kanlıca on the Asian side just after the bridge, and

yoghurt sellers usually embark to sell you the famous Kanlıca yoghurt, eaten with a spoonful of sugar.

Kanlica to Sariyer

Above the bridge, the districts on the European side are wealthy residential areas and you will see many magnificent mansions on the shoreline. The district of **Tarabya** is famous for its many fish restaurants and the best hotel on the Bosporus, the Büyük Tarabya.

The next stop is at **Sarıyer**, an attractive fishing village whose seafront is lined with tall houses in elaborate designs, some wooden, some brick, all in multitudinous colours.

The final leg

From Sarıyer the boat crosses to the Asian side for the last stop at **Anadolu Kavağı**, where visitors can take their pick of the many fish restaurants. After lunch climb the hill to the Genoese castle on the summit for a fine sweeping view across the straits out to the so-called Clashing Rocks that mark the exit of the Black Sea, and which Jason and the Argonauts had to navigate on their search for the Golden Fleece.

LOTS OF CHOICE

Ticket touts are numerous along the waterfront but not all tours make all stops mentioned in the text. If you especially want to visit any attractions, make sure the boat stops there before buying your ticket.

By boat: The Bosporus

Alexander: the Greeks in Turkey

The arrival of Alexander the Great on the ancient scene opened a new era in history, and especially for what is now Turkey. At the tender age of 21 Alexander crossed the Hellespont in 334 BC at the head of an army of about 35,000 Macedonians and Greeks, with the express goal of liberating the Greek cities of Asia Minor and conquering the Persian Empire. He achieved his aim with remarkable speed, encountering the mysterious Gordian knot on the way (the ancient city of Gordion lies 106km (66 miles) west of Ankara). This was the knot that the Phrygian King Gordius had tied to fix the yoke to the pole of his ox-cart, and an oracle had foretold that whoever undid it would be master of Asia.

The ruins of Perge, one of Alexander's first conquests on the road to Persia

Alexander the Great, as pictured by a Renaissance artist

Having heard of the legend, Alexander felt obliged to fulfil the prophecy. He took one look and simply sliced the knot through with his sword. Within 18 months he had retaken Anatolia and within three years had conquered the entire Persian Empire.

Alexander died in Babylon at 32 from a sudden fever. (It was said afterwards that his short way of dealing with the Gordian knot had fulfilled the prophecy but condemned him never to enjoy the fruits of his conquest.) His vast, newly acquired empire was left without an heir. His generals proceeded to squabble among themselves for 20 years and finally three main kingdoms emerged: the Macedonians in Greece, the Seleucids in Syria and the Ptolemies in Egypt.

His conquest, however, created a corridor linking Greece to Persia and the East, a corridor down which ideas could travel and cross-fertilise, sowing the seeds for a tremendous flowering of thought and scholastic achievement that was to transform the civilised world. It was known as the Hellenistic period and lasted 1,000 years.

The Aegean coast

Arguably Turkey's most beautiful region, the Aegean coast is an area of rolling hills and fertile valleys covered in cypress and pine trees, olive groves and vineyards. Even 2,500 years ago the famous historian Herodotus maintained it was blessed with the best climate in the world, and in summer there is always a gentle breeze to temper the fierce heat. The coastline is magnificent, indented with endless bays and inlets. Now an army of tourists follows in the footsteps of Greeks, Romans and early Christians, and though some pockets along the coast are heavily developed, it is still possible to travel beyond the resorts and find deserted beaches and unspoilt rural villages.

Maybe it was the beauty of these surroundings that encouraged the flowering here of brilliant civilisations. After the fall of Troy around 1250 BC, several waves of Greek emigrants came and settled, founding cities and producing great scientists, historians and poets like Homer.

The greatest of these ancient cities were Ephesus and Miletos, but throughout the Aegean region there are, literally, hundreds of ancient cities, the ruins of which can still be visited and explored.

Afrodisias (Aphrodisias)

A generation ago this ruined Greek city was regarded as an attractive but unexciting site. All this was changed by one man, Professor Kenan Erim, who devoted his life to excavating the site between 1961 and 1990. His efforts have transformed the once buried ruins into a showpiece city that rivals Ephesus in its grandeur. His own tomb now lies within the ruins.

Inland, 166km (103 miles) from Kuşadası, off the Aydın–Denizli Rd. Open: daily 8.30am–6.30pm. Admission charge.

Museum

Here you can admire the fine statues found on the site, many of Aphrodite, goddess of the city. She was originally an indigenous fertility goddess, later becoming the Greek Olympian goddess of love and beauty. Aphrodisias was famous in antiquity for its school of sculpture, using the exquisite marble, often blue in colour, quarried from the local hills.

Theatre complex

The path from the museum leads first to the theatre, in front of which is an *agora* (marketplace) with a magnificent colonnade of blue marble columns, and then to the large theatre baths beyond.

Baths of Hadrian and sports complex

The path leads over a hill and down to a plunge pool with a handsome black-and-white paved courtyard to one side, and the large Baths of Hadrian to the other.

Odeon and Bishop's Palace

Passing through the poplar-treed field, which used to be the city's main marketplace, you reach a charming little odeon (theatre) dating from the 2nd century AD, one of the most perfect structures of its kind in all Asia Minor. Beside it is the unusual building known as the Bishop's Palace, with a courtyard of lovely blue marble columns.

Temple of Aphrodite

The path leads on to the huge Temple of Aphrodite which is thought to date from 100 BC. Many well-preserved Ionic columns are still standing. In the late 5th century, the temple was converted to a Christian basilica.

Stadium

Beyond the temple lies the magnificent Stadium, one of the best preserved in the Greco-Roman world, with a capacity of 30,000.

Monumental gateway and Sebasteion

Returning in a loop back towards the museum, the path leads past the monumental gateway, with its lovely spiral fluted columns, and on to the mysterious building called the Sebasteion, which encloses a processional way.

Ruins of the monumental gateway at Aphrodisias

Ayvalık

Until the 1920s Ayvalık was a centre of Greek commerce, a bustling market town benefiting from its role as a port for wine and olive oil from the island of Lesvos just offshore.

Today the bustle is still evident – especially on market day (Thursday), and trade with Lesvos (now Greek territory) continues in the form of day boat trips for tourists.

The waterfront is a lively place where fresh seafood is sold from numerous stalls. Just inland the nucleus of the old town remains, with its wrought-iron balconies just one sign of an elegance now fading but still full of character.

Ayvalık has no beach in town, but to the south swathes of fine sand are now backed by a collection of tourist hotels that constitute the modern resort, the largest along the Turkish northern Aegean coast.

160km (100 miles) north of Izmir.

Behramkale (Assos)

This fishing village, with an attractive waterfront, lies at the foot of an acropolis (a hilltop city centre), where the ruins of Assos stand facing out to sea. It offers a few renovated old hotels, which are popular with the artistic and literary community from Istanbul. On the approach to the village is a fine 14th-century Seljuk bridge. Ancient Assos has impressive fortified walls, and the Temple of Athena, right on the summit, is the oldest Doric temple to have survived in Asia Minor.

93km (58 miles) south of Çanakkale, 73km (45 miles) south of Troy. Open: daily 8.30am–5.30pm. Admission charge.

Bodrum (Halicarnassus)

Bodrum is one of the liveliest resorts in the Aegean, Turkey's St-Tropez. A high-rise building ban has ensured that Bodrum's low-rise, bohemian-style, white-bungalow character remains unchanged. Its atmosphere leans more towards European Mediterranean than Turkish, and it has a certain ritziness in its bustle that is not found in most Turkish resorts. The resort boasts some of the best entertainment and nightlife in the country.

Bodrum itself has no beaches and so a number of beach resorts have grown up on the peninsula beyond, such as **Gümbet** (the biggest), **Turgutreis** and **Gümüşlük**, all of which can easily use Bodrum as the lively centre.

Bodrum, ancient Halicarnassus, was famous in antiquity as the site of the Mausoleum, one of the Seven Wonders of the World. Nothing of this remains today beyond a few foundation blocks and a hole in the ground, but Bodrum is famed now instead for its role as the premier Aegean yachting centre, and for its fine Crusader castle.

Bodrum lies at the end of a peninsula, 174km (108 miles) south of Kuşadası, 195km (121 miles) north of Marmaris, three hours' drive from Izmir or 40 minutes from Bodrum/Milas airport.

The ancient remains

Most of ancient Halicarnassus lies buried under the modern town, and part of the charm of Bodrum today lies in stumbling across bits of ancient masonry set in the walls, used as door stops or lying about in gardens. Above the town, largely overgrown, is the ancient theatre, which the energetic can climb up to for a fine view over the harbour.

The famous Mausoleum, the magnificent tomb built by Queen Artemisia for her husband Mausolus in the 4th century BC, stood for 1,700 years and was finally destroyed by earthquakes. When the Crusader Knights arrived in 1402 they used its remains as a quarry to build their castle. It lives on in this, and in the modern word it has given us.

Castle of St Peter

This is one of the last and finest examples of Crusader architecture in the east, magnificently preserved and in a spectacular setting on a promontory guarding the harbour.

The Knights Hospitaller of Rhodes built the castle around 1402, after the Mongol leader Tamerlane destroyed their previous fortress in Izmir. But when Süleyman the Magnificent conquered their base on Rhodes in 1522, the knights were obliged to withdraw to Malta, abandoning the castle. The castle is home to the impressive Museum of Underwater Archaeology, with several medieval

vaulted halls displaying finds from the Bronze Age to the Byzantine era, discovered by divers in the waters offshore. To explore the whole thing at leisure takes two hours, and several open-air cafés encourage lingering. *Open: daily 8.30am–noon & 1–5pm. Admission charge.*

Dalyan (Caunus)

The fishing village of Dalyan, site of ancient Caunus, has been discovered in a big way recently, largely through the publicity of naturalist David Bellamy's 'Save the Loggerhead Turtle' campaign. It has burgeoned into a bustling place with many hotels, and tourists are asked to swim from the other end of the long beach to avoid damage to turtle eggs.

A visit to ancient Caunus, reachable only by boat from the promenade, is a special experience (*see pp66–7*). *Dalyan lies 10km (6 miles) off a side road from the main Marmaris–Fethiye road, south of Lake Köyceğiz.*

The Castle of St Peter at Bodrun

Aegean coast

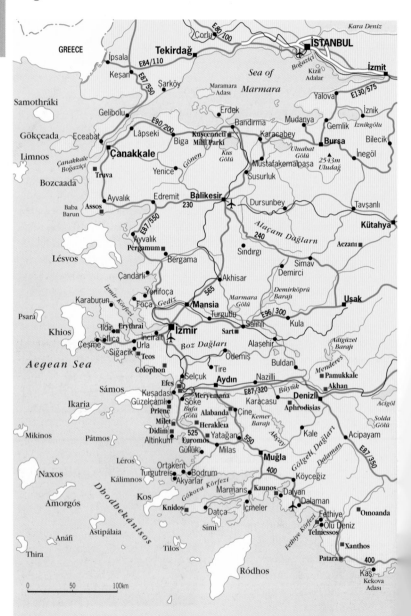

BIBLICAL TURKEY

The Old Testament

In Genesis, Mount Ararat is cited as the final resting place of Noah's Ark after the flood: 'And after the end of the hundred and fifty days the waters were abated. And the Ark rested on the seventh month, on the seventeenth day of the month, upon the mountains of Ararat.' Hopeful Christians make regular expeditions up the mountain in search of evidence for the existence of the Ark, which some scientists claim to have found.

The biblical Ur of the Chaldees is the modern town of Urfa (Şanlı Urfa), home of Abraham, before he was called 'to go forth into the land of Canaan'. He stopped off in Harran for several years until he was 75, and 1km (²/₃ mile) northwest of Harran is a well-known spot called Jacob's Well, Bir Yakub. Was it here that Jacob was said to have kissed Rachel, and Rebecca later to marry Isaac, drew water for Abraham's servant?

The New Testament

Christianity took root very early in Asia Minor, with St Peter the Apostle founding the first Christian community in Antioch around AD 47. It was here that the followers of Jesus were first called Christians, and the Acts of the Apostles describe how the disciples met for teaching, communal prayer and the breaking of bread. These were also the first congregations to include Gentiles as well as Jews.

Ephesus became the principal centre of Christianity in Asia Minor in AD 53, with the arrival of St Paul, who stayed for three years. He left and later wrote his letters to the Ephesians, the most profound of his Epistles. St John the Evangelist lived in Ephesus from AD 37 to 48, accompanied, so many assert, by the Virgin Mary, whose tomb is claimed to be in the hills 7km (4¹/₂ miles) south of Ephesus. John returned to Ephesus later still to write his Gospel, and died here in AD 95.

The Aegean coast

he coastline at Dalyan with its beautiful crescent beach

Dalyan boat trips

A boat trip on the Dalyan River offers one of the most varied tours in Turkey and in many ways captures the essence of what this country has to offer: nature at its best and rarest, ancient remains, beautiful beaches, together with New Age therapeutic cleansing (or just a chance to mess about in the mud, depending on your point of view) before the day is out.

Boats depart from the quayside at Dalyan village, from where you can already get a magnificent view of the ancient Lycian tombs cut high into the sheer cliffs on the opposite bank. These are some of the finest in the region, made more dramatic by their setting.

The boats move with ease past the verdant reed beds that crowd the riverbanks. These house a wealth of wading birds and constitute an important breeding ground for herons and storks. Downstream the boats stop at a small jetty where you'll disembark to visit the site of ancient Caunus.

The town was set on a high bluff offering fantastic views to the sea. In Roman times, the slow-draining river

A boat passes the Lycian rock tombs in Dalyan

Enjoy a thermal mud bath

basin (leading from Lake Köyceğiz) and marshy surroundings meant malaria was a constant threat to the citizens of Caunus, yet they still created all the trappings of a successful city including a large amphitheatre – the city made its money from the slave trade.

Where the river meets the sea, nature has worked another bit of magic – Istuzu Beach. This magnificent sand spit makes for excellent sunbathing but is also a protected turtle nesting zone. Between May and July is the time to keep your eyes open just offshore to spot female turtles returning from the depths of the ocean to lay their eggs.

After allowing you to enjoy the beach for a few hours, your boat will take you back upstream to the shores of Lake Köyceğiz where you can 'get down and dirty' in the mud baths at Ilıca. Turks believe this slightly smelly green/brown paste will cure just about anything, but for most holidaymakers it's just a lot of fun.

On the return to Dalyan you get the chance to swim in Lake Köyceğiz, its cool fresh water a refreshing contrast to the salty Mediterranean.

The street leading to the theatre in Ephesus

Efes (Ephesus)

Showpiece of Aegean Turkey, Ephesus today is visited daily by thousands. Sacred city of Artemis, famous throughout history for its temple, which was one of the Seven Wonders of the World, Ephesus also boasts many magnificent Roman remains from the time when it was capital of the Roman province of Asia.

17km (10½ miles) north of Kuşadası on the road to Selçuk, a 45-minute drive from Izmir. Open: daily 8am–6.30pm. Admission charge. Temple of Artemis open: daily 8.30am–6.30pm. Admission charge. Slope House admission separate.

Temple of Artemis

The greatest temple in all Asia Minor, originally four times greater in area than the Parthenon, it was built to venerate Artemis of the Ephesians, a Greek adaptation of the Anatolian earth-mother, whose outstanding quality was her fertility, depicted in her statues by the rows of breasts hanging from her chest. On her annual feast day orgies were held here. The cult was continued by the Romans, identifying her with their own fertility goddess Diana, and the temple was the object of pilgrimage for more than 1,000 years, conferring great wealth on the city. The solitary temple column that rises today from a muddy pool is a challenge to most visitors' powers of imagination.

Main Ephesus site

Though not blessed with a spectacular setting like either Pergamum or Priene, Ephesus' unique interest lies in its completeness as a city. Walking along its magnificent white marble streets flanked with colonnades, shops, civic buildings and the houses of the wealthy it is perhaps easier here than in any other Greco-Roman city to relive its past grandeurs.

Theatre

From the site entrance, head straight for the theatre and climb to the top seats for an overview of the city. Most of the ruins that lie before you date from the Roman imperial age, when the population was about 250,000. The seating capacity of the theatre is 25,000, and it is still used for performances during the annual Festival (*see p18*). St Paul preached here, and the acoustics today are as excellent as they were then.

Library of Celsus

Standing at the end of the Marble Street, this library is the best-preserved structure of its kind, named after Celsus, Proconsul of Asia in AD 106, and whose tomb is inside it.

Behind the library is the massive Temple of Serapis, part of the Egyptian bull cult.

Downtown Ephesus

Beyond the library the street which snakes uphill (Curetes Street) leads into what is regarded as downtown Ephesus, with wealthy Romans' apartments to the right and public buildings to the left. Do not miss the communal latrines and the brothels in this left area. To the right is Slope House, a three-storey Roman mansion whose mosaic floors and wall murals have been renovated to offer a glimpse of interior design Roman style. Though it is an extra ticket fee, the added dimension it gives of the reality of human existence here (albeit for the wealthy few) is well worth it.

The ancient Library of Celsus at Ephesus

Izmir (Smyrna)

Izmir, Turkey's third-largest city, was ancient Greece's Smyrna. A large Greek community thrived in the city until the 1920s, when Izmir was the scene of interracial violence following the founding of the Turkish Republic. When Greeks and Turks exchanged populations, most Greeks moved west across the Aegean.

The highlights of the remains of ancient Smyrna are the ancient Acropolis and the Roman Agora set on a flat-topped hill, the Kadifekale. Finds from the site, and others in the region, are presented in the Archaeological Museum, and there is an interesting Ethnological Museum that focuses on the later Ottoman era.

Izmir environs

Çeşme

The most famous of the beach resorts around Izmir, Çeşme is a well-established resort and thermal spa, with long, sheltered sandy beaches, several holiday villages and the full range of water sports. It is an attractive fishing town with a relaxed atmosphere, and the harbour is dominated by a splendid 14th-century Genoese fortress. Behind the fortress is a labyrinth of twisting backstreets, and along the promenade is a myriad of seafront restaurants of varying quality.

The excellent beaches lie a little outside the town, but are easily accessible by taxi or *dolmuş* (shared taxi running on a regular route).

A ferry runs twice weekly to the Greek island of Chios (Khios) 14km (8¹/₂ miles) offshore. The journey takes one hour (*see pp142–3, p144*).
80km (50 miles) west of Izmir,
90 minutes' drive from Izmir airport.

Foça

This pretty fishing village, with its cobbled streets and whitewashed houses, is still a very Turkish place, with just a few hotels beside the beach. The Club Med has a holiday village nearby.
45km (28 miles) northwest of Izmir,
50 minutes' drive from Izmir airport.

Sart (Sardes)

Sardes was the ancient capital of the Lydian Empire under King Croesus, he of the legendary wealth. Founded 5,000 years ago close to a gold seam, the city soon became extremely rich, giving rise to the mythical stories of its most famous ruler.

The recently renovated buildings are few but of extremely high quality. The

Richly carved friezes adorn the Roman gymnasium at Sart

Roman gymnasium complex has an exceptional façade with fluted columns and richly carved friezes on pediments and cornices re-erected by archaeologists to its 3rd-century AD design. Sadly, once inside the complex the other rooms lie in ruins.

One kilometre (²/₃ mile) north of the gymnasium complex lie the remains of the Temple of Artemis, a 6th-century BC edifice, which was one of the largest in the ancient Greek world. The temple platform and few columns that remain are enough to give an impression of the immense scale.

90km (56 miles) east of Izmir on the E23 to Uşak. Open: daily 8.30am–5.30pm. Admission charge.

Sığacık

This seaside village is a pretty spot with a fine Genoese fortress dominating its harbour. On the headland 2km (1¹/₄ miles) beyond it are some lovely sheltered bays with camping and hotels. The ancient site of Teos lies nearby in the olive groves.

45km (28 miles) southwest of Izmir.

Kuşadası (Bird Island)

Trebled in size in the last ten years, Kuşadası is now Aegean Turkey's major resort, a bustling town set in a wide bay. What it offers is a lively centre for entertainment and nightlife, and a good location as a base for excursions, notably to nearby Ephesus.

Its name comes from the island at the end of the bay, now linked to the mainland by a concrete causeway. The Genoese fortress on the island still guards the harbour. Besides its yacht marina, Kuşadası is also a port of call for Aegean cruise ships, and boats run daily to the Greek island of Sámos opposite.

There is a small public beach on the main bay, but the sandy beach at Kadınlar Plajı (Ladies' Beach), 3km (2 miles) from the centre, is preferable. The bazaar offers a fine selection of jewellery and clothing, and there are more restaurants clustered together in the town and seafront than you could ever sample.

94km (58 miles) south of Izmir, 17km (10¹/₂ miles) southwest of Ephesus, 174km (108 miles) north of Bodrum on the coast opposite Sámos. One-hour transfer to Izmir airport.

Kuşadası environs
Altınkum

A long and safe, sandy beach has been Altınkum's main selling point. It's now a burgeoning family resort with a mainly British clientele but makes a smaller and lower-key alternative to Kuşadası.

60km (37 miles) south of Kuşadası.

SMYRNA'S WINE

Ancient Smyrna (Izmir) was famous for its wine, which Homer tells us was drunk sweet and mixed with honey, chalk and powdered marble. On top of this, it was diluted five parts to two with water. To drink wine neat was considered quite barbaric.

Didim (Didyma)

Associated above all with its magnificent Medusa's heads, Didyma is the name of the great temple precinct of Apollo's oracle, famous throughout antiquity for its predictions. The oracle itself was located in the innermost chamber of the temple, tended by the chief priest and the priestesses. Christianity spelt the end of the oracle racket. Emperor Theodosius announced in AD 385 'No mortal man shall have the effrontery to encourage vain hopes by the inspection of entrails, or which is worse, to attempt to learn the future by the detestable consultation of oracles'.

Today it is still possible to imagine the temple's splendour. A phalanx of marble Corinthian columns stood at its entrance, guarding the inner sanctum, which is reached down two short dark passages. Over 100 other columns' base lie *in situ* around the structure.
56km (35 miles) south of Kuşadası. Open: daily, winter 8.30am–6.30pm; summer 8.30am–7.30pm. Admission charge.

Efes (Ephesus)

See pp68–9.

Milet (Miletos)

A great ancient sea-trading city that rivalled Ephesus at its peak, Miletos is well worth a visit. Its prosperity was based on its four sheltered harbours, difficult to imagine now, as the sea is 8km (5 miles) away as a result of the Maeander river valley silting up. The process is ongoing, and the Aegean is getting further away at the rate of 6m (6 1/2 yds) a year. The site is extensive, and the major monument is the theatre, perhaps the most outstanding of the over-200 Greco-Roman theatres in Turkey. Look out as well for the Roman Baths of Faustina, with walls still over 15m (49ft) high.
63km (39 miles) south of Kuşadası, 133km (83 miles) north of Bodrum, 26km (16 miles) south of Priene and 19km (12 miles) north of Didyma. Open daily, winter 8.30am–6.30pm; summer 8.30am–7.30pm. Admission charge.

Priene

Reminiscent in some ways of a miniature Delphi, the ancient city of Priene is very Greek, with none of the grandiose Roman monuments that abound

Medusa's head, Didim

elsewhere. It boasts a spectacular setting, perched up in the lee of a vast rock outcrop, and its layout was devised by the pioneering town planner Hippodamus, who created a series of intersecting streets to form a grid pattern – a model taken for granted by today's architects.

Note the interesting quarter of private houses, where it is said Alexander the Great stayed before his visit to consult the oracle at Didyma. There is also a charming Greek theatre shaded by pine trees. From here a path leads up the rocky outcrop to the sanctuary of Demeter, from where there are superb views.

26km (16 miles) north of Milet, 42km (26 miles) south of Kuşadası and 44km (27 miles) north of Didyma. Open: winter 8.30am–6.30pm, summer 8.30am–7.30pm. Admission charge.

Selçuk

The modern town of Selçuk sits cheek by jowl with Efes (*see p68*); in fact, the stones of its major buildings were plundered from the once great Roman city. Here you'll find the **Efes Museum**, repository of the finest artefacts discovered at the site. The museum is laid out in a series of themed rooms and galleries – the first re-creates daily life in a Roman villa, using genuine artefacts. Pay particular attention to the array of small personal articles on display, from fine jewellery to cooking pots to glass vessels. The colossal

statuary gracing the galleries is impressive. Look particularly for several of Artemis, the multi-breasted, wide-hipped representation of fertility.

Standing atop the highest ground in Selçuk is an imposing medieval fortress (now closed to the public). In its shadow rest the remains of one of the most important sites of early Christianity, the **Basilica of St John**. Though it is difficult to imagine now, this church once matched Ayasofya in Istanbul in size and splendour. The tomb of St John the Evangelist lies at the site.

Seven kilometres (4¹/₂ miles) from the centre of Selçuk is another site revered by both Christians and Muslims. **Meryemana** is said to be the place where the Virgin settled after leaving the Holy Land in the aftermath of the Crucifixion. Discovered in this wooded vale in 1891 after a nun in Germany had a vision of it, the diminutive chapel on the site was proved by scientists to have foundations dating from the 1st century AD. Today it is a place of pilgrimage, particularly on the Feast of the Assumption (15 Aug).

Efes Museum: Agora Carsısı. Open: Tue–Sun 8am–noon & 1.30–5.30pm. Admission charge. Basilica of St John: St John Sokak. Open: daily 8am–7pm. Admission charge. Meryemana: 7km (4¹/₂ miles) south of Selçuk. Open: daily dawn–dusk. Free admission, but parking fee.

Drive: Menderes Valley

This 160km (99-mile) drive starts at the coastal resort of Kuşadası and takes in the central Aegean's most majestic ancient sites whilst driving through beautiful landscapes, before ending with a swim at one of its finest beaches. There are lots of small cafés along the route for snacks, though it is wise to take water with you so you don't dehydrate when you are sightseeing.

Allow 10 hours (a full day) including sites and museums.

Leave Kuşadası and travel towards Selçuk on route 515. Two kilometres (1¼ miles) before the town you'll find the turning to Efes (Ephesus) on your right.

1 Efes (Ephesus)

If you arrive at Efes before 10am you'll have the place pretty much to yourselves, but 10am signals the arrival of squadrons of tour buses.

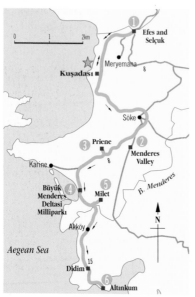

Across the main road from the site are the scant remains of the Temple of Artemis, once one of the Seven Wonders of the World.

Head into Selçuk itself to visit the Efes Museum (*see p73*), where the best of the excavated finds are on display. Then head to St John's Basilica and Meryemana (7km/4½ miles from town) before returning to Selçuk for a well-deserved lunch.
From Selçuk take 515 south, bypassing Kuşadası and following signs for Söke. Take the Söke bypass (signposted Bodrum) rather than going through town. As you leave town you'll see a green mosque on the right and take the right turning just beyond that (signposted Priene and Milet).

2 Menderes Valley

The river snakes its way somnolently towards the Mediterranean (its ancient name gave us the word 'meander') still depositing 6m (20ft) of silt every year. It's a richly fertile area, with crops of sunflowers, cotton and vegetables offering contrasting colourful images throughout the year.

Just after the village of Güllübahçe take the turn right for Priene.

3 Priene

Come here for majestic views and a taste of interesting town-planning ideas dating from 350 BC.

Continue on the same road. After 9km (5½ miles) there is a left fork signposted to Didim. Take this route to head south into the protected area of the delta.

4 Büyük Menderes Deltasi Milli Parkı

The park protects vast tracts of salt flats and coastal shallows, the ideal environment for native and migratory birds such as storks, herons and flamingoes. The local Turks flock here for pole fishing.

After you cross the Menderes itself you'll see signs left for Milet.

5 Milet

The great Greco-Roman city of Miletos, where the theatre is the masterwork.

Continue through the village of Akköy to Didim, where the temple of Didyma appears on the right on a tight bend in the road.

6 Altınkum

From Didim head 4km (2½ miles) south to Altınkum for a cooling swim and relax on the beach, where there are lots of bars and cafés for a refreshing drink before you return to Kuşadası.

Take a right at Akköy and then a left at the junction with route 525 for the quickest route back, retracing your route from Söke.

A woman leads her cow in the Menderes Valley

Marmaris

Set in a huge fjord-like bay with pine forests reaching right down to the sea, Marmaris is one of Turkey's most attractive resorts. After Bodrum, Marmaris is the Aegean's main yachting centre and embarkation point for boating holidays, but it retains a much more Turkish feel to it than Bodrum.

The harbour promenade is enjoyable for strolling, and the older part of the town, with its excellent bazaar, is a pedestrian precinct lined with colourful restaurants and cafés. Unlike Bodrum, Marmaris has a good town beach, but you can take a *dolmuş* or a water taxi to numerous pretty bays nearby. Most of the larger hotels are in **İçmeler** (8km/ 5 miles to the west), with its fine shingle beach kept immaculately clean, or at **Turunç** (9km/5½ miles to the south), again with a safe, sandy bay. Both places are linked to Marmaris by a cheap and regular water taxi.

Marmaris is a 90-minute drive from Dalaman or Bodrum airport, 61km (38 miles) south from Muğla, off the main Muğla–Dalaman Rd.

Marmaris environs

Datça

A fishing village that is now a resort and was once the site of old Knidos (Cnidos).

75km (47 miles) west of Marmaris.

Knidos (Cnidos)

Right at the tip of the peninsula, Cnidos can be a day's outing by boat or by car. It has attractive Greco-Roman ruins in a fine setting on a headland, and offers swimming and some simple fish restaurants.

107km (66 miles) west Marmaris.
Open: daily 8.30am–sunset.
Admission charge.

Sanctuary of Zeus at Labranda

Milas

Set in a fertile plain surrounded by wooded mountains, Milas (ancient Mylasa) is a busy town on a natural crossroads, its river banks lined with once lovely but now decaying Ottoman mansions. Before the Ottomans, the local dynasty called the Menteşe emirs ruled here from their castle stronghold **Beçin Kale**. This dramatic castle is visible from miles around on the dramatic flat-topped mountain just south of Milas. This splendid fortress was in use by the local governor until the 17th century, and can still be visited today.

72km (45 miles) northeast of Bodrum, 131km (81 miles) northwest of Marmaris and 71km (44 miles) west of Muğla. Open: daily 8.30am–6pm. Admission charge.

Milas environs

Bafa Gölü (Lake Bafa)

This beautiful lake makes a good stopping place for lunch on day trips in the area, with its simple lakeside fish restaurants. The evocative ruins of ancient **Herakleia** lie on the opposite shore, approachable by a small track.

30km (18¹/₂ miles) northwest of Milas.

Euromos

You cannot miss the elegant columns of this temple by the roadside. It dates from the 2nd century AD and is one of Asia Minor's best-preserved temples.

15km (9¹/₂ miles) north of Milas on the way to Lake Bafa. Open: daily 8.30am–6pm. Admission charge.

Ruins of an ancient Greek temple in Euromos

Labranda

Set high in the hills above Milas, this is the site of a sanctuary to Zeus. It is an impressive site, excavated by the Swedes since 1969.

17km (10¹/₂ miles) north of Milas. Open: daily 8.30am–6pm. Admission charge.

Muğla

Set on a plateau, the town of Muğla is the capital of Muğla Province and was also the capital of the Menteşe emirs in the 16th century. The old quarter lies to the north of the main road and it makes a pleasant change from all the Greco-Roman sites to wander in the bazaar and the winding lanes with their attractive Ottoman houses.

135km (84 miles) east of Bodrum, 73km (45 miles) north of Marmaris.

Muğla environs

Alinda (Karpuzlu) and Alabanda

A visit to these two ruined cities makes an interesting day trip. Alinda is remarkably preserved, in spite of never having been excavated, with the finest Greek market building in the country.

60km (37 miles) north of Muğla on the road to Aydın.

The limestone pools at Pamukkale

Pamukkale

Even though the spot is now highly commercialised, Pamukkale is a unique natural wonder and will leave an unforgettable impression. A bizarre network of fantastical open-air white stalactite rock formations and hot springs, its name means 'Cotton Castle', a graphic description of the white terraces tumbling down the hillside. The limestone deposits in the water are continuously building on to the structure, and it has taken 14,000 years for them to reach their current state.

Turks themselves, always keen on natural wonders, are very fond of the place, and it is a popular day's outing from far around. Stalls selling cheap souvenirs abound and the atmosphere is always festive. Its popularity became its downfall as too many people clambered over the pools and bathed in the water, contaminating it with suntan oils. Large hotels built atop the hill siphoned off the mineral-rich water for their swimming pools leaving little to replenish the pools, many of which lost their lustre.

Today it is forbidden to bathe in the pools and the hotels atop the hill are gone. Water flows again over the cascade and the pools are returning to their glistening white. One narrow channel has been left for visitors to walk up through the pools, but without shoes, making it hard work for smooth feet.

Pamukkale's hot springs were credited from the first with religious and mystical qualities, so early cities grew up here centred round the springs. The ancient city that is still in evidence behind the Cotton Castle is called Hierapolis (Holy City) and dates from Roman times.

If you are fortunate enough to be spending the night at Pamukkale, it is pleasant to stroll round the extensive remains at dusk or even by moonlight. The vaulted baths have been turned into a museum (9am–5pm).

The major monument in terms of size is the large Roman theatre with its well-preserved stage building. Beyond this, the road leads out through the monumental northern gateway to reach the vast necropolis, one of the most extensive in all Asia Minor. Over 1,200 sarcophagi have been counted, all lining the beginning of the ancient route to Ephesus.

217km (135 miles) east of Kuşadası, off the main E24 road, and 17km (10½ miles) north of Denizli. Pamukkale is a three-hour drive from Kuşadası. The whole area never shuts but there is an admission charge to enter the main site, designated a national park, and a parking fee.

Pamukkale environs
Akhan

Just 1 km (²/₃ mile) after the turn-off to Pamukkale on the road east towards Dinar stands an impressive Seljuk caravanserai faced in pinkish marble – traditional overnight accommodation for travelling merchants.

There are at least 50 of these handsome buildings on the main trade routes of central Anatolia, all built in the 13th century when the Seljuk Turks were the dominant power in Anatolia.

BU YOL YALNIZ
YALINAYAK YÜRÜYÜŞ ve
FOTOĞRAF ÇEKMEK İÇİNDİR
ONLY FOR WALKING WITHOUT
SHOES AND TAKING PHOTOS

Cryptic signage at the edge of the pool

Colours of the rainbow in Pamukkale's rock formations

Turkish carpets

Hand finishing a carpet

Carpet weaving is a great Turkish tradition begun by the nomadic Seljuks in the 12th century. Their art recalled their nomadic background, for the carpet is the essential piece of tent furniture.

There are three categories of rug: the knotted pile carpets (*hali*), flat weaves (*kilim*) characterised by their lack of pile and their rug-like size, and the silks, which are in a class of their own. These are the most expensive and the most luxurious, and the fineness of the silk yarn allows the weaver to create minute detail in the rich colours. *Kilims* were traditionally made by women for use at home, not for sale. Patterns and colours were therefore not dictated by commercial expediency but were reflections of the weaver's identity, her family and her tribe. Most *kilims* are sheep's wool,

Anatolian women plying their skills, converting fleece into yarn

Displayed wares in the Covered Bazaar, Istanbul

but some are goat hair and cotton. In the home they were used as floor covering but also as wall hangings, door curtains, prayer rugs, large bags for cushions and saddlebags, and small bags for salt, bread, grain or clothing.

Natural dyes were traditionally made from roots, bark, berries, vegetables and minerals. Then in the second half of the 19th century aniline chemical dyes were introduced and their use has gradually replaced most of the old vegetable dyes. Pink and orange were never found in natural substances, so the presence of these or any other colour with a harsher brightness indicates chemical dyes. Today's weavers invariably use chemical dyes for convenience, and

have therefore been freed from the constraints of plant availability in their area which in the past led to certain dominant colours in certain areas, such as Turcoman red and Balıkesir blue and red. The designs and patterns also give clues to the region, though it takes years of practice to identify carpets correctly. A few designs are common to all areas, notably the prayer rug with its solid arch-shaped block of colour representing the *mihrab* (prayer niche) that faces Mecca in a mosque wall. Prayer rugs were used exclusively for prayer, and the symbols to look out for on them are the hands of prayer, the mosque lamp, the tree of life, the water jug, the jewel of Muhammad or the star of Abraham.

Pergamum

Pergamum is one of Turkey's most impressive sites by virtue of its striking setting on a steep acropolis. At its peak in the 2nd century BC, Pergamum rivalled Alexandria as a centre of learning and science, with a famous library building, the remnants of which can still be seen on the acropolis. In an act of eccentricity, the last Pergamum king bequeathed his entire kingdom to Rome, thus hastening the advent of Roman influence in Asia Minor.

Pergamum is next to the town of Bergama, 3km (1³/₄ miles) off the E87 coast road from Çanakkale to Izmir. It is 197km (122 miles) north of Izmir and 243km (151 miles) south of Çanakkale. Site open: daily 8.30am–5.30pm. Admission charge.

Acropolis and theatre

German archaeologists have reconstructed many of the buildings on this fine citadel, including five kings' palaces, the famous library and the temple of Athena, patroness of learning. The Pergamum library was said to have contained 200,000 books, written for the first time on animal skins, known as 'pergamum paper', from which the English word parchment comes. Mark Antony, to please Cleopatra, presented the entire Pergamene library to Alexandria, where books had always been written on papyrus. The theatre, built into the steep hillside, is a remarkable piece of Hellenistic engineering.

A reconstruction of the fabled Wooden Horse, the downfall of an unsuspecting Troy

Asklepieion

Set down below the acropolis are the remains of a remarkable medical centre dedicated to Asklepius, god of healing. This popular centre was based upon the fame of Galen, the greatest physician of late antiquity, born here in AD 129. Some patients stayed here as long as a year. One Roman patient, suffering from indigestion, was put on a diet of bread and cheese with parsley and lettuce, told to go barefoot and take a run each day, to coat himself with mud and anoint himself with wine before entering a hot bath. A grateful inscription tells us his treatment was successful.

Red Basilica

In the old Turkish quarter of Bergama stands this colossal red-brick Byzantine basilica, originally a Roman temple to the Egyptian bull god of Serapis. A fine Roman three-arched bridge spans the river nearby.

Truva (Troy)

Troy is a city that lives in the imagination through Homer's tales in the Iliad and the Odyssey. To find that it really exists comes as a surprise to many, but far from being the mighty city of Helen and King Priam, it is today a series of shapeless mounds and ditches with occasional outcrops of wall and foundation. In an attempt to make up for the lack of exciting remains, the authorities have constructed an enormous wooden horse at the site entrance. Children can climb up inside this to relive the legendary climax of the siege of Troy when the Greeks tricked their way inside the city walls.

Heinrich Schliemann was the German businessman and amateur archaeologist whose romantic childhood obsession with Troy first led to its rediscovery. He obtained permission from the Ottoman sultan to excavate here in 1870, using money he had amassed in the California gold rush, and spent the next 20 years of his life pursuing his dream. He was rewarded with the discovery of four Troys, one on top of the other, and the so-called Jewels of Helen, in which his wife posed for newspapers and which Schliemann kept until bequeathing them to the Berlin Museum.

Today there are thought to have been a total of nine Troys, layer upon layer. Which one was Homer's Troy is the subject of a modern Trojan war, with Troy VI and Troy VII as the main contenders.

As you walk round the small site, all the various levels are labelled, but the whole nevertheless comes across as very confusing.

5km (3 miles) off the E24 coast road between Çanakkale and Ayvacık and 32km (20 miles) southwest of Çanakkale. Open: 8.30am–5.30pm. Admission charge.

Ruins of the ancient citadel at Pergamum

Mediterranean Turkey

Turkey's southern shore has to rank as one of the most beautiful coastlines anywhere in the Mediterranean. It stretches for some 600km (373 miles) from Fethiye in the west right through to Iskenderun near the Syrian border. The coastline falls into several distinct regions, so varied that as you pass from one to another it is almost like entering a different country. The whole length, however, shares the benefit of an excellent climate with 300 days of sunshine each year.

The first region, from Fethiye to Kemer, is called **Lycia**, also known as the Turquoise Coast, with the wildest and most dramatic coastal scenery in Turkey. The mountains tumble right down to the sea and there are glorious sandy beaches and spectacular ruined cities to explore.

The next region, from Antalya to Side, is **Pamphylia**, a flat fertile coastal plain with the mountains set further back from the sea.

From Alanya, the region that extends to the Syrian border is called **Cilicia**, the western section of which runs round the headland to Silifke and is rugged and beautiful but sparsely populated. The coastal drive is magnificent but tiring. The Cilician plain from Mersin to Iskenderun is the least interesting part of this coast, with flat river valleys and industrial sprawl around Adana.

Adana

Set on the banks of the Seyhan River, Adana, Turkey's fourth-largest city, is the centre of a rich agricultural region

and of the prosperous cotton industry. However, apart from its 16-arch Roman bridge and its covered bazaar, the only building of note in the city is the Ulu Camii (Great Mosque), built in 1507 from black and white marble on Abidin Paşa Caddesi in the city centre.

The city has several good hotels and makes a good base for visiting nearby sites.

Adana environs
Dilekkaya (Anavarza)

The ruins of this lovely Roman

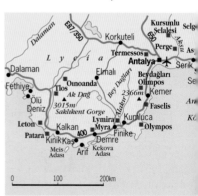

Byzantine city include a stadium, tombs, an aqueduct, a theatre and several basilicas.

30km (18½ miles) north from Ceyhan, 72km (45 miles) northeast from Adana.
Open: always. Free admission.

Karatepe

A striking Hittite site in the mountains with many fine sculptures.

77km (45 miles) north from Ceyhan, 129km (80 miles) northeast from Adana.
Open: daily 8.30am–5.30pm.
Admission charge.

Kızkalesi (Maiden's Castle)

A 12th-century Armenian castle, 100m (110yds) offshore, with fine beaches nearby. It is difficult to visit.

122km (76 miles) southwest from Adana on the E24.

Silifke

A pleasant town on the banks of the Göksu River overlooked by the Crusader Castle on its acropolis, from where there are fine views. A 15-minute drive further

east are the curious caves of Cennet and Cehennem (Heaven and Hell).

161km (100 miles) southwest from Adana on the E24.

Tarsus

Once a charming town with old houses and gardens, famous as the place where Antony first met Cleopatra, and the birthplace of St Paul, whose original name was Saul of Tarsus.

42km (26 miles) west of Adana on the E5.

Uzuncaburç (Diocaesarea)

A pretty village surrounded by the Roman ruins of a theatre, temples and a tall Hellenistic tower.

38km (24 miles) north of Silifke.

Yakapinar (Misis)

The site of superb Roman mosaics.

28km (17 miles) east of Adana. Open: daily 9am–5pm. Admission charge.

Yılanlıkale (Castle of the Snake)

An imposing eight-towered, 13th-century Armenian castle.

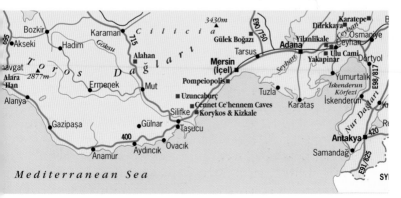

6km (4 miles) east of Ceyhan on the road to Gaziantep, 48km (30 miles) east of Adana. Open: always. Free admission.

Alanya

A modern beach resort and ancient Seljuk city, Alanya's prominent feature is its mighty rock, which juts out Gibraltar-like into the sea. On top is its amazing red-brick crenellated fortress (red bricks were the favoured building material of the Seljuks), and below, on either side, are magnificent sandy beaches with the modern town and its many hotels.

The fortress with its 150 towers enclosed the 13th-century town built by the Seljuk sultan Keykubad I, who used it as his winter quarters and naval base. The outer wall is 7km (4¹/₂ miles) long and took 12 years to build. The walk up from the modern town takes about 40 minutes, so many may prefer to take a taxi, particularly on a hot summer's day. Within the walls you

Red Tower near the sea at Alanya

can explore old gateways, Byzantine chapels, the dilapidated residential quarter, mosques, a *bedestan* (covered market) and caravanserai and the citadel at the very summit. Surrounding the citadel, within the upper walls, is the pretty village of Ehmediye, its whitewashed houses now home to tearooms or the backdrop to displays of linen and embroidery for sale.

In the old Seljuk dockyard area below the rock stands the colossal Kızıl Kule (Red Tower), built to defend the port in 1226. From this port area you can hire small boats to explore the many grottoes which honeycomb the base of the Alanya rock.

131km (81 miles) east of Antalya on the E24. Open: always. Free admission. Citadel open: Tue–Sun, Apr–Oct 9am–7pm; Nov–Mar 9am–5pm.

Anamur

The rugged landscape all around the headland of Anamur was notorious for piracy and brigandage in ancient times, and many ruined fortresses litter the coast. The best preserved and largest of these is Anamur, a Crusader castle with all its walls and 36 towers still standing. Right on the beach with the waves lapping its walls, it dominates the surrounding plain and was the foothold on the mainland for the Lusignan kings of Cyprus, which is less than 80km (50 miles) away. Inside you can climb stairways up many of the towers.

Two kilometres (1¹/₄ miles) west of the castle the ruins of a Byzantine city

Fortifications of the castle at Anamur

called **Anemurium** cover the hillside, with traces of mosaic and painting in the private houses (it is always open to the public, admission free).

3km (1¾ miles) east of Anamur town on the E24. Anamur castle is open daily 8.30am–5.30pm. Admission charge.

Antakya (Antioch)

Until 1939 Antakya and this curious pocket of land known as the Hatay in the southeast corner of the Mediterranean belonged to Syria, but the French gave it to Turkey in exchange for support against Germany in World War II. Set in pleasantly hilly countryside, Antakya lies on the Orontes River. In Roman times, as ancient Antioch, it was a notorious centre of good living, not to say depravity, and it is the remnants from those days which make the town worth visiting today. These take the form of Roman mosaics from the floors of private houses, the finest collection in the world. Dating from the 2nd and 3rd centuries AD, they are displayed in the **Hatay Archaeological Museum**. Besides the museum, the town has an old

Roman bridge over the river and a picturesque bazaar quarter.

193km (120 miles) southeast of Adana on the E5, 104km (65 miles) west of Aleppo. Museum open: Tue–Sun 8.30am–noon & 1.30–5pm. Admission charge.

Antakya environs
Harbiye (Daphne)

This was Antioch's pleasure suburb where most of the lavish villas were situated, and where Apollo's pursuit of the nymph Daphne is said to have taken place. The laurel into which she turned herself still grows all around. Nothing remains of the buildings, but the gardens and streams are still a popular picnic site for the locals.

Samandağ

From Antakya it is a 30-minute drive to this beautiful sandy beach, near which are the ruins of **Seleucia Persia**, the ancient port of Antioch, once one of the greatest ports in the Mediterranean.

ALARA HAN

About 39km (24 miles) northwest along the main coast road from Alanya a sign points inland to Alara Han, an unusual Seljuk caravanserai with a richly carved main door. This inn for merchants is one of seven along the road from Konya and Alanya, standing a day's walk apart from each other. Alara Han is now fully restored and open as a museum cum bar/restaurant, offering Turkish folklore evenings (*open: 9am–11pm; admission charge*).

On the hill top north of it stands the breathtaking Seljuk fortress. It takes a good hour to climb to the summit (*Open: always. Free admission*).

Mediterranean Turkey

Antalya

This is the major resort of Mediterranean Turkey, a city rather than a town, with its own airport and industrial port as well as a modern yachting marina. What is more, it has been the main port on Turkey's south coast for the last 2,000 years. During the Crusades, the Christian armies sailed for the Holy Land from here to avoid the long and difficult march across Anatolia. There is a small shingly beach in front of the restored old quarter. However, the best beaches are at Lara, 12km (7½ miles) east, where you will find that many hotels are concentrated.

Karaalı Park

On the clifftops on the road to Lara, this park offers spectacular views towards the mountains of Lycia. It also has a little zoo and some good cliff-edge restaurants.

Museum

Here statues, sarcophagi and mosaics from the ancient cities of the coastal plain, notably Perge, are on display. The wealth of artefacts from the monumental to the mundane will really help you picture the daily life of the people as you visit sites such as Aspendos, Perge and Termessos.

Located on the western outskirts of town, on the main road to Kemer.
Open: Tue–Sun 8am–noon & 1.30–5pm.
Closed: Mon. Free admission.

Old port and marina

Kaleiçi, as the old town is known, is the prettiest part of Antalya, with elaborately carved Ottoman houses clustered on the steep, winding cobbled lanes. There has been a settlement here for over 2,000 years, growing up around the natural harbour at the foot of the hill. The Romans fortified the harbour, and during the Ottoman era it was surrounded by strong walls 5km (3 miles) long. The Ottoman city had four separate districts for Greeks, Jews, Muslims and the ruling Mameluke clan After the founding of the Turkish Republic all foreigners left and Kaleiçi was almost abandoned. The 1980s brought a renaissance of the old mansions – now housing restaurants, bijou hotels and boutiques.

Yivli Minare (The Fluted Minaret)

This is Antalya's most prominent monument, built of the distinctive Seljuk red brick in the 13th century.

Antalya environs
Aspendos

Here is the finest example of a Roman theatre, indeed of any ancient theatre, anywhere in the world. Aspendos cannot fail to impress. Built in the 2nd century AD and renovated on the orders of Atatürk, the perfect structure serves today as a venue for wrestling matches and theatrical performances. Climb the hill behind the theatre for excellent views into the auditorium. You'll also see unexcavated remnants of a city; the most impressive buildings being a fine Roman aqueduct and an early basilica.

49km (30 miles) east of Antalya, off the E24 and 36km (22 miles) west of Side. Open: daily 8.30am–5.30pm. Admission charge.

Düden Şelalesi (Düden waterfalls)

These are a spectacular sight where the Düden River cascades into the sea.

10km (6 miles) from Antalya on the Lara road.

Ionian columns at Perge

Kurşunlu Şelalesi (Kurşunlu waterfalls)

Impressive waterfalls.

18km (11 miles) north of Antalya on the Isparta road.

Perge

Here stand the extensive ruins of a Hellenistic/Roman city. Having no defences, it submitted immediately to Alexander the Great on his way to Persia. Perge has been heavily excavated since 1946, and the major monuments are the theatre, with some fine carved reliefs, the stadium, the best preserved in Turkey after that of Aphrodisias, with seating for 12,000 spectators, and the circular Hellenistic gate towers built from golden stone, that lead into the main colonnaded street where chariot ruts can still be seen. This street was cooled by water which flowed down a channel at the centre – a kind of early air-conditioning for the shops located here. You can examine what remains of their fine mosaic floors.

18km (11 miles) east of Antalya, 2km (1¹/₄ miles) north of the main E24 coast road. Open: daily 8.30am–5.30pm. Admission charge.

Termessos

A visit to Termessos, known as the Eagle's Nest, is one of the most exciting excursions in Turkey. It takes a good half day to explore, great fun even if ruins do not inspire you. Built in the 4th century BC by a people of legendary fierceness and independence, it is a city set high on pine-clad mountains, now a designated national park.

Exploring the site involves a lot of climbing and walking, so comfortable footwear is important. A network of waymarked paths leads all over. Particular highlights not to be missed are the gymnasium, the theatre and the necropolis or cemetery.

34km (21 miles) northwest of Antalya, off the road to Korkuteli. Reached only by car or taxi. Open: daily 8.30am–6.30pm. Admission charge.

Walk: Selge Canyon

This drive and walk gives the chance for visitors who are based in a coastal resort like Side or Alanya to sample the delights of inland Turkey, with the ruined ancient city of Selge as the final goal. The scenery is magnificent throughout, with gorges and mountains, a striking contrast to the flatness of the coastal plain. In the heat of summer it can provide a pleasant escape, as the air is noticeably cooler than on the coast and there is a constant breeze. Selge itself lies at an altitude of 1,000m (3,280ft).

The trip should be regarded as a full day's excursion from your base, and after driving to reach the starting point, the amount of walking is up to you, and can be anything from one to six hours.

Selge is reached by turning off the main E24 coast road between Side and Antalya, at the signpost marked Beflkonak and Köprülükanyon Milliparkı (National Park of the Canyon with the Bridge). The total drive from Side is 90km (56 miles) and takes about 80 minutes, through pretty wooded foothills with glimpses of the wide Eurymedon River below. Beyond Beşkonak the road continues for a further 6km (3½ miles) to reach the famous Roman bridge over the canyon, starting point for the hugely popular white-water rafting trips.

Roman bridge

The starting point of the full walk is the Roman bridge, a superb construction across the canyon and river, as sound today as the day it was built. Just before the bridge is a series of restaurants serving a speciality of delicious river trout, a welcome stop for refreshment on your return. Touts may try to persuade you to take the river trip.

An impressive feat of early engineering, the Roman bridge spanning the Eurymedon River

Driving or walking according to time and preference, follow the sign to Altınkaya (14km/8½ miles), which forks left after the restaurant to lead across the bridge, then forks right.

Fairy chimneys

The narrow road zigzags steeply to climb the 700m (765yds) from the bridge, and as you near the plateau where the village of Altınkaya and the ruins of Selge lie, you will notice weird rock formations called fairy chimneys, the result of wind erosion. There are fabulous precipitous views across the mountains and valleys, with no habitation anywhere until the cultivated fields around the village are reached. The fairy chimneys are a good place to leave the car if you want a much more leisurely walk, as it takes about 15 minutes from here to reach Selge.

Altınkaya and ancient Selge

As you approach, the ancient theatre rises imposingly behind the village with a backdrop of snow-covered mountains. The track leads through the village and climbs up to reach the theatre from behind, so that you pop straight on to the top seats, which offer wonderful views. The contrast between what must have been a flourishing city and the poverty of the village seen today could hardly be more striking. The village children are charming and invariably insist on accompanying you on your tour for a small fee. Ancient capitals and marble blocks now humbly

Still waters in the rocky Köprülu Canyon en route to Selge

serve as garden furniture in the yards of village houses.

From the top of the theatre a path leads off to the west along the ridge of the hill and leads through foundations and tumbled columns to what seems to have been the ancient main street with evidence of the drainage system underneath. This street leads to the *agora*, paved in fine flagstones with much ancient carving scattered about, including a lovely white marble bull's head. On the hillock beyond the *agora* are the remains of a Christian basilica from the days when Selge was the seat of a bishop in Byzantine times.

A scramble down the front of this hillside gives a view of the ancient city walls. Rejoin the track beside the old Roman spring, where a small amount of drinkable water still trickles out.

Elmalı

This still-unspoilt Turkish town lies
at the heart of a vast apple-growing
region (Elmalı means 'place of the
apples'). The lifestyle of the people here
is simple, separated as they are from the
coast by two ranges of hills. Highlights
of the town are the main mosque and
the old town, where numerous
Ottoman mansions flank narrow old
cobbled streets.

90km (56 miles) inland from Kaş.

Fethiye

Fethiye lies on the western edge of the
wild region known as Lycia. It is fast
becoming one of Turkey's most popular
tourist areas because of its magnificent
mountain scenery and beaches, its
stunning ancient remains and its
closeness to both Dalaman and Antalya
airports. Set in a wide, open bay backed
with mountains, Fethiye is a bustling
town, Lycia's main port and fishing
centre. Its wide promenade is lined
with café-bars as it rounds the
colourful harbour and small yacht
marina. The cobbled streets inland are
busy with shops and restaurants, and
the daily open-air market is always
crowded. There are several discos and
nightlife is lively. The town itself has no
beach, but Çalış bay is a long sand and
pebble beach 4km (2½ miles) away.

Fethiye boasts ancient remains in the
group of rock-cut temple tombs in the
cliff face above the town, reached by
climbing lots of steps. On the summit
itself is a crumbling Crusader fortress.

In front of the town hall stands an
enormous sarcophagus, one of Lycia's
finest, left here by the two earthquakes
of 1956 and 1957.

Fethiye environs
Kaya (Kayaköy)

This is a unique Greek ghost town
abandoned in 1923 when the exchange
of Greek and Turkish minorities took
place and all the 3,500 Greeks returned
to Greece. Covering three hillsides, it is
an eerie experience to walk round the
decaying houses. The fading frescoes of
Panagia Pyrgiotissa church are worth
seeking out.

Some houses at the bottom of
Kayaköy village have been bought and
restored, housing atmospheric cafés,
souvenir shops or B&Bs. Stay into
the evening and you'll almost have the
town to yourself.

5km (3 miles) from Fethiye,
off the Ölü Deniz Rd.

Ölü Deniz

See p103.

Saklıkent Gorge

Water has carved this 18km (11-mile)
gorge into the red and gold striated
sandstone of the Ak Dağlar Mountains,
leaving behind a whimsical landscape
of smooth rounded bulges, bowls
and bluffs. You can walk for 2km (1¼
miles) into the gorge across the stream
of very cold water coursing from a
fissure close to the entrance. At the
mouth of the gorge are several cafés

erving river trout (farmed) and
urkish snacks, with tables overhanging
he water.
0km (31 miles) east of Fethiye.

los

his is the site of an ancient Lycian city
n a splendid setting high on a rocky
romontory above the Xanthos (Eşen)
alley. Heavily overgrown and never
xcavated, Tlos is a charming place to
xplore, with an acropolis fort, a
heatre, baths and unusual cliff tombs.
*5km (11 miles) from Kemer, which is
*2km (13¹/2 miles) east of Fethiye, the
rack is signposted just after crossing the
ridge in Kemer. Open: 8.30am–6.30pm.
Admission charge.*

inike

Centre of the local tomato and orange
roduction, Finike is a busy agricultural
own rather than a resort. Its
interland, however, holds several
nteresting excursions.
*18km (73 miles) southwest of Antalya,
82km (113 miles) southeast of Fethiye.*

inike environs
Arif (Arykanda)
This is a lovely Lycian ruined city, set
igh in the mountains, in the lee of
a cliff face overlooking a beautiful
orested valley. There is lots to explore –
he temple tombs, the baths,
gymnasium, theatre and the stadium.
*5km (21¹/2 miles) north of Finike on the
Elmalı Road. Open: daily 8.30am–5.30pm.
Admission charge.*

Kale (Myra)
Formerly known as Demre, this dusty
town lies on a flat alluvial plain where
tomatoes grow in profusion under
plastic sheeting. Set into the hilly
outcrop at the back of the town is the
ancient city of Myra. Its most important
site is a superbly preserved Roman
theatre, behind which is a network of
rock-cut tombs, some of which bear
impressive reliefs of funeral banquets.

A separate extensive necropolis of
rock-cut tombs lies 2km (1¹/4 miles)
to the east on a track, which includes
the so-called Painted Tomb, one
of the most remarkable in all Lycia.

Another surprise in store back in
the centre of town is the church of
St Nicholas set down in a sunken
hollow. Nicholas, born in Patara, a few
kilometres away, was Bishop of Myra in
the 3rd century AD and was endowed
with miraculous powers. His cult has
come down to us today in the form of
Santa Claus (St Nicholas), answerer of
children's prayers.

Visit the beach where the river flows
out into the sea, now called Çayağzı,
formerly Myra's ancient port of
Andriake. A cluster of fish restaurants
awaits you. The huge stone building at
the side of the estuary is the ruined
Roman granary.
*46km (28¹/2 miles) east of Kaş, 27km
(17 miles) west of Finike. Tombs open:
daily 8.30am–5.30pm. Admission charge.
St Nicholas open: daily, May–Oct
9am–7pm; Nov–Apr 9am–5pm.
Admission charge.*

Mediterranean Turkey

Walk: Cadyanda, Lycia

This excursion offers the chance to see some of Lycia's magnificent mountain scenery, well away from the crowds of the coast, culminating in a climb to Cadyanda, a little known ancient hilltop city. You can walk along easy forest tracks for an hour or so to reach the summit, and then spend an hour exploring the picturesquely overgrown ruins of Cadyanda.

Allow half a day for the whole outing from Fethiye, but could easily make a relaxing day trip too.

To reach Cadyanda, drive from Fethiye on the main coast road to Marmaris, then fork off inland after 3km (1¾ miles) towards Üzümlü, 20km (12½ miles) to the north.

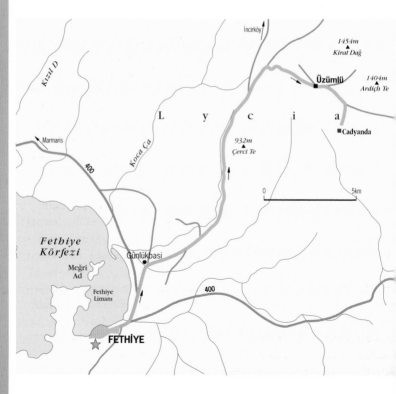

Üzümlü

At the village the tarmac ends, but a drivable track continues and Cadyanda is marked on a yellow sign pointing straight out beyond the village.

Leaving your car by the domed cistern in the fields 600m (650yds) beyond the village, the walk up the forest track to reach the ancient city of Cadyanda takes just over an hour. If you want to shorten the walk, drive on to the highest point of the track, where there is a little parking area, and from where it is only half an hour's walk to the top.

Dramatic views

The scenery all around is magnificent – Lycian landscapes in all their majesty. The forested hills drop away to the Xanthos valley and beyond it rise the distant peaks of Ak Dağ, the White Mountain.

The necropolis

Take the wide path from the parking area that seems to lead a little downhill at first, and this will lead you after 30 minutes or less to a wide-open necropolis area of Roman stone-built tombs, some with carving round their doors.

The theatre

Above the necropolis, through the trees, you will notice a steep earthy slope that ends in the remains of the city walls of Cadyanda, and immediately behind them lies the charmingly rustic theatre,

A Roman stone carving in the necropolis

with trees growing up through the seats. The pit dug in the centre of the semicircle is the work of a hopeful treasure-seeker – in all parts of rural Turkey villagers were convinced that ancient ruins contained treasure. Why else would foreigners spend so long poking around among these old stones?

The city centre

Climbing to the top of the theatre, a small path can be found that leads up through the forest past some vast open cisterns still full of stagnant water, to the centre of the city, where you will find the baths, the largest buildings still standing, and a big stadium, heavily grassed over but with seats intact along one side. The setting, in a grassy clearing in the forest, is tranquil and relaxing; an excellent picnic spot.

By boat: Kekova

This outing in a boat makes an enjoyable and relaxing day, combining a swim and a simple lunch out at a village restaurant with a visit to several ancient Lycian cities in and around the island of Kekova about 30km (18½ miles) from Kaş. Some of the cities are partly underwater as a result of earthquakes over the centuries. Tickets for the trip can be bought from Kaş harbour, and the boat leaves at 9am, returning around 6pm.

Allow one day.

Carpets and rugs drying in the sun on Kekova

Off season, or if you find that you have missed the large boat, you can negotiate a price with any fisherman in the harbour to take you instead. This is obviously more expensive, but has the advantage that you can dictate the timing. Boats to visit Kekova can also be hired from Çayağzı, the harbour of Kale (Demre), a little further to the east, actually a lot closer to Kekova than Kaş. Currently swimming and snorkelling are not permitted in Kekova Sound. Check at the time of booking, and if the answer is yes, don't forget your swimwear and snorkel for better views of the underwater ruins.

As the boat leaves Kaş harbour, it first passes the island of Meis Adası (Kastellorizo), then, after about 90 minutes, the ruins of Aperlae, a Lycian town dating from the 4th century BC.

Aperlae

The spot is uninhabited now and the nearest village is an hour's walk inland.

The town walls are the best-preserved remains at Aperlae, and in the shallow water of the bay your captain will point out whole streets and the outline of buildings now submerged.

Tersane

A further 45 minutes' cruising brings you to a lovely cove on Kekova Island, with a Byzantine church apse standing just offshore. This is called Tersane.

The boat skirts the edge of Kekova Island, where rock-cut stairways, house foundations and the occasional door lintel can be made out underwater. Then it heads across to the mainland.

Simena

The ancient site of Simena stands above the current village of Kale (castle), named after the Byzantine fort with its crenellated walls on the summit. This is an excellent place to haggle over the price of a Turkish carpet or some hand-made lace sold by the ladies of the village. Lunch is generally taken at one of the simple restaurants here in the harbour overlooking more submerged ruins and the occasional Lycian sarcophagus standing in the water.

After lunch it is worth climbing up through the village to the fort to find the charming, tiny rock-cut theatre set near the summit. More huge sarcophagi, so typical of Lycia, are scattered about the hillsides.

The boat journey back to Kaş takes about 2½ hours. From Çayağzı it is only about an hour, but fewer boats run as there are less people to fill them.

Kale on Kekova Island, with the fort on the hill to the left

Tea

Tea vessel

Despite Turkish coffee being famed around the world – it was this short strong brew that spawned the espresso – it is tea that keeps the Turks going. They consume the equivalent of 3kg (6½lbs) per year for every man, woman and child.

That the country is self-sufficient in tea is probably one reason for its popularity. The region around Trabzon on the eastern Black Sea coast has over 65,000 hectares (160,000 acres) under cultivation and very little of it leaves the country.

Tea oils the works of daily life. Served in delicate tulip-shaped glasses, without milk, it is light and

A lovely clear brew of Turkish tea

efreshing. Most Turks inject a shot of energy by adding liberal amounts of sugar to the glass.

Tea also plays an important role in commerce. It will be served at the start of a business meeting when the parties will engage in small talk – it's considered rude to jump straight into matters at hand. It's the same in the carpet shop. Once the rugs are rolled out for your perusal you'll be invited to take tea. This is partly a tradition of Muslim hospitality and partly an acknowledgement that the buying process is longer and the negotiations more complicated than in the west. Haggling over the price of goods – not a natural situation for western shoppers – is supposed to be an enjoyable, not stressful, process.

Tea is never brewed on the premises. Numerous little cafés dot the bazaars in Turkey and an order is swiftly dispatched. Your tea will arrive within minutes on a silver tray, carried by a tea boy. The same boy will return after your transaction has been completed to take away the empties.

In the evenings there's nothing that Turks like better than to sit chatting and smoking their *narghiles* over several glasses of tea. The low tables and bench seats covered in carpets and *kilims* found at traditional cafés such as those close to the Blue Mosque in Sultanahmet or on the

Serving tea the traditional way

narrow streets of Kaş) are a link back to their nomadic roots, when everything had to be carried on camel-back. Once you get used to the different seating position, this is really a most relaxing and comfortable way to spend an hour or two.

TURKISH CUSTOM

The preparation and serving of tea continues to be one area where the sexes are separated. At home it is the women who control the kitchen. A man would never interfere in this female arena to make his own tea.

The cafés, however, are the domain of men, owned and operated solely by men, and pride is taken in this most traditional occupation.

Limyra

Famous for Lycia's most extensive necropolis, the ancient site of Limyra boasts a theatre, a Byzantine nunnery, and the remarkable tomb of Pericles, a local dynast, which is set high on a rocky platform overlooking the plain.

8km (5 miles) north of Finike off the Elmalı road. Open: always.
Free admission.

Kalkan

A traditional fishing village with a growing number of small hotels and pensions, Kalkan is also a frequent stop for flotillas and yachts. The beaches are man-made. There is a small rocky one in the harbour, but the rest are a short boat ride away, complete with pool and sunbathing terrace. The steep slopes on which the village itself is built run right down to the rocky harbour. Boats also run to nearby bays for secluded swimming. Many of the pensions have idyllic roof terraces where breakfast is served in the mornings, and then they turn into lively bars in the evenings. With its attractive setting, cobbled winding lanes and slightly up-market

feel, Kalkan makes a good base for explorations inland.

25km (15½ miles) west of Kaş, 22km (13½ miles) southwest of Xanthos.

Kalkan environs
Kınık (Xanthos)

Always the greatest city of ancient Lycia, Xanthos is a magnificent site on a hill top overlooking the Eşen Çayı (Xanthos River). Renowned for their courage, the Xanthians were twice slaughtered in defence of their city.

Seventy crates full of sculptures and inscriptions from the city were shipped off to the British Museum by the archaeologist, Charles Fellows, in 1842. The extraordinary pillar tombs beside the theatre date to the 5th and 4th centuries BC. The excavated ruins are extensive and a visit involves quite a lot of scrambling about on small goat paths. Behind the theatre you will find the acropolis with the king's palace and a rock-cut pool. Further afield a Byzantine basilica can be found with a mosaic floor, and a cluster of rock-cut tombs near the necropolis.

45km (28 miles) northwest of Kaş, 64km (40 miles) southeast of Fethiye. Open: daily 8.30am–5pm. Admission charge.

Leton (Letoon)

This pretty site is the sanctuary of Leto, mother of Artemis and Apollo, where ancient festivals of Lycia used to be held. Much of the sanctuary lies underwater today, alive with frogs and tortoises, giving it a special charm.

LYCIAN TOMBS

Lycia's chief legacy is its tombs. They have survived earthquakes, the ravages of battle and pillaging, and are remarkable today for their sheer profusion, their size and their often dramatic settings cut into cliff faces, littered over hillsides or even submerged in the sea. Many pre-date Alexander the Great.

4km (2½ miles) off the main
Fethiye–Kaş road, 4km (2½ miles) south
of Eşen and 26km (16 miles) from
Kalkan. Open: daily 8.30am–5.30pm.
Admission charge.

Patara

Patara boasts a superb sandy beach
22km (13½ miles) long, which is
protected because it is a turtle nesting
area. The nearby tourist village of
Gelemiş, has a few basic hotels, but the
authorities are attempting to limit
further development. It is only a village
today, but in antiquity, before it sanded
up, it was Lycia's port, where the
Xanthos River meets the sea. The
ancient city has seen little excavation,
and it is charming now to discover the
theatre half-submerged in sand, and the
occasional overgrown temple. The most
imposing building of all is also the most
difficult to reach, the vast long granary
of Hadrian, where local grain was stored
before being shipped back to Rome.
7km (4¼ miles) south of Xanthos. The
beach is 1km (⅔ mile) beyond the site.
Open: daily 8.30am–5.30pm.
Admission charge.

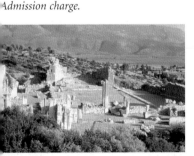
The Byzantine basilica at Xanthos

Kaş

This is Lycia's most popular resort with
many small hotels and quite a chic
harbour-front lined with cafés and
restaurants. Set in a lovely bay enclosed
by high mountains all around, the
Greek island of Meis Adası (Kastellorizo)
lies directly opposite. The harbour at
Kaş is bustling, and offers its own daily
boat trips to nearby attractions. The
main bay does not have a swimming
beach, but there are small rocky
swimming areas to both sides of the
bay where the town has spread, many of
which have been claimed by adjacent
hotels or campsites. They are not
suitable for young children. Local
fishermen run an efficient and cheap
water-taxi service to take you off
to any favoured bay, returning to
collect you later.

Modern Kaş occupies the site of
ancient Antiphellus, and the remains of
that Lycian city can be seen in the small
theatre above the town and in some
fine sarcophagi scattered about in the
town and harbour.
109km (68 miles) southeast of Fethiye,
73km (45 miles) west of Finike.

Kaş environs
Kekova Adası (Kekova Island)
See pp96–7.

Meis Adası (Kastellorizo)
Once the finest harbour between Piraeus
and Beirut, this island can be reached by
a 40-minute boat ride from Kaş.

Mediterranean Turkey

Kemer

Kemer is a busy and popular family resort which has remained low-rise, so the feel is still of a small town rather than a concrete jungle. The beaches are good, both sand and shingle, and kept immaculately clean. There is a bustling marina, and the Moonlight Beach complex (open to the public for a small admission charge) offers excellent sports and water sports. At the Yürük (Nomad) Theme Park you can watch traditional craftwork in action. The shops sell carpets and other goods of excellent quality and the place has quite a sophisticated atmosphere. The setting, backed by Lycia's high mountains, is superb. Kemer is also well placed for sorties to Lycia's antiquities or to Antalya.

30km (18¹/2 miles) south of Antalya.

Kemer environs
Faselis (Phaselis)

This is an ancient Lycian city which has remains to explore from the Roman era. It has three natural harbour bays where swimming is a delight. The pine-covered slopes drop right down to the shoreline, giving lots of shade in the tree-covered ruins, where you can explore the main paved street, the theatre and baths, and the aqueduct just metres from the water's edge. Sarcophagi are scattered about here and there in the undergrowth.

13km (8 miles) south of Kemer, 57km (35 miles) south of Antalya. Open: daily 8.30am–5.30pm. Admission charge.

Olimpos (Olympos)

Now set within its own national park, this ancient ruined city takes its name from Mount Olympos, and the whole district is heavily wooded and mountainous. A river estuary meets the sea at Olympos and the valley is overgrown with pink oleander bushes tumbling in profusion everywhere.

Olympos has never been excavated, but enthusiasts can find in the undergrowth a theatre, baths, a basilica and temple. The pebble beaches provide excellent swimming. A short drive or long walk from the beach takes you to the mountainside, where flames leap out spontaneously. Referred to as *ateş* locally, meaning fire, this was held in antiquity to be the site of the Chimaera, the fire-breathing monster of the underworld.

31km (19 miles) south of Phaselis, 44km (27¹/2 miles) south of Kemer. Open: daily 8.30am–5.30pm. Admission charge.

Ölü Deniz (Dead Sea)

This lagoon offers Turkey's most beautiful beach (and busiest), encircled by high pine-clad mountains which plunge straight down into the turquoise sea. Though the lagoon is now designated a conservation area, there are many small hotels and restaurants down on the beach itself. The bulk of the accommodation, however, is 4km (2¹/2 miles) inland in busy resorts like Ovacik and Hisarönü, linked by cheap and frequent *dolmuş* taxis.

Temple of Apollo at Side. Although the city was Greek in origin, most of its ruins are Roman

Boats can be hired from the beach to explore the island of **Gemili** with its Byzantine churches and the Blue Cave. Yachts are not allowed to enter the lagoon itself.

17km (10¹/₂ miles) south of Fethiye.
Open: daily 8am–6pm.
Admission charge to the lagoon itself.

Side

Side is unique in that the modern resort is actually set among the ruins of the ancient city in between long stretches of sandy beach. It offers a host of hotels, motels, pensions, campsites and restaurants, yet despite all the development, the old town centre has retained its own identity. It has long been a favourite with Turks as well as foreigners, so its atmosphere is that of a genuine, lively Turkish resort, less spoilt than Marmaris or Kuşadası. The old town sits on a small traffic-free promontory. The stroll across the it from one beach to the other takes you through the old Roman city, mingled with the town of red-tiled roofs and narrow stone-walled alleyways. The shops offer a fine selection of souvenirs especially in jewellery, onyx and carpets.

Of all the ancient cities on Turkey's southern shore, Side is the only one to have been systematically excavated. The city flourished under the Roman Empire, and most of the extant monuments date from that period. The splendid theatre, seating 17,000, is one of the largest in Asia Minor, and the top seats afford splendid views over the *agora*, museum, baths and temples, and to the beaches beyond.

73km (45 miles) east of Antalya, 66km (41 miles) west of Alanya on the E24 coast road. Site museum open: Tue–Sun 8.30am–5.30pm. Admission charge.

Side environs
Manavgat Şelalesi
(Manavgat waterfalls)

A lovely spot for lunch in summer, the waterfalls are more like rushing rapids than true falls. A series of souvenir shops heralds the approach, and inside the fenced-off area an extensive restaurant is laid out with some tables perched up on individual platforms in the rushing water itself.

7km (4¹/₂ miles) northeast of Side up a signposted fork off the E24 coast road. Open: daily 8.30am–6pm. Admission charge.

Selge
See pp90–91.

Drive: Turquoise Coast

Only completed in the 1980s, this 280km (174-mile) road hugs the precipitous cliffs of the Turquoise Coast offering magnificent views throughout the route. You'll be tantalised at the sight of tiny beaches lapped by azure water before the route zigzags through forests heady with the fragrance of pine and resonant with the humming of cicadas. This drive would make an ideal transfer from Fethiye to Antalya but you may want to extend the journey to two, three or more days as the resorts mentioned are particularly alluring as night falls.

Allow 10 hours (a full day) including stops.

Set out east from Fethiye on route 400. The road runs inland for the first section of the trip, skirting the Baba Dağ mountain range then cutting south again along the wide, sweeping coastal plain to Kınık, one of the finest cities in antiquity, much of which is now in the British Museum in London.

1 Kınık (Xanthos)

After Xanthos, you'll begin to notice a great increase in plastic-covered cloches that seem to blanket the fields. You are now entering Turkey's main tomato production region. You may also have to avoid tomatoes that fall from lorries laden with the fruit for market! Turn

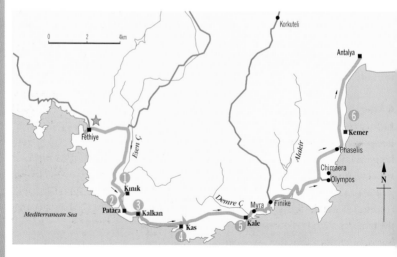

right at the signs for Gelemiş/ Patara and take care on the 7km (4½-mile) road that leads to the site, as farm animals may wander across your path.

2 Patara

Patara's beach is one of the best in Turkey, protected from development because it is a nesting site for turtles. Just inland is the ancient city, now choked by sand and suffocated by tussock grasses, though still a delight to explore.

3 Kalkan

Kalkan (30km/18½ miles east) was once a tiny fishing village but is now an up-market resort with some excellent small hotels.

The section of the route leading from Kalkan to Kaş is probably the most spectacular as the road switchbacks around cliffs that rise directly out of the water. Magnificent views catch the eye, though there are few places to stop for that all-important photograph. The tiny white beaches look so inviting and attract yachts and *gülets* to enjoy the ultimate form of peace and quiet on the water.

4 Kaş

Kaş is the jewel of the Turquoise Coast. Before tourism was established it was a hippy hangout with no road access and still retains touches of its bohemian past with some excellent bars, restaurants and shopping – this may be the place to break the journey for lunch, or for the night.

5 Kale (Myra)

On the road approaching Kaş, and between Kaş and Myra to the east, watch out for ancient Lycian tombs standing sentinel in olive groves. Myra has a particularly fine collection of rock-cut tombs, plus the early Byzantine basilica dedicated to St Nicholas – the man we know as Santa Claus.

From Myra the mountains retreat a little and the scenery is not as impressive until after Finike, when the road climbs between two mountain ranges through dramatic forested peaks. To the south a still secret corner of Turkey, with the sites of Olympos and Chimaera, lies down unmade roads, but carry on, plunging back down to the water's edge to the ancient site of Phaselis amongst pine trees and golden beaches.

6 Kemer

The modern resort of Kemer lies a little way north. Apart from its beaches there's little to hold you here, especially as the delights of Kaleiçi, the old town of Antalya, await, with fine restaurants and cobbled alleyways filled with interesting boutiques.

Tourists enjoy shopping at Kaş

Anatolia

Anatolia, the heartland of Turkey, is largely bleak and inhospitable, a plateau over 1,000m (3,300ft) high, that alternates between the bitter cold of winter and scorching hot of summer. The national capital, Ankara, straddles the divide between the cosmopolitan west and the colossal Asian landmass to the east.

Ankara

Ankara is a curious city. As modern Turkey's capital it has many roles to play, and it is the conflict of these roles that makes the city so intriguing. Set in the heart of the Anatolian plateau, it was chosen by Atatürk in a deliberate move away from the Byzantine and Ottoman associations of Istanbul.

The city is set within a basin on a series of small, steep hills. The wide main boulevards run in straight lines along the open valleys, while the narrow side streets zigzag uphill. Here are the houses of the rural immigrants, huddled together covering every inch of ground, painted in blues, greens, mauves and yellows, where

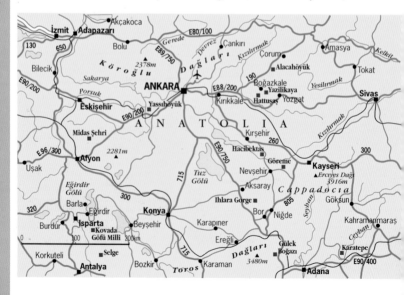

the bulk of Ankara's 4 million population lives.

Though it is Turkey's new capital, Ankara is far from being a new city. The main streets are lined with luxury high-rise hotels, European-style restaurants and cafés, impressive new embassies and government buildings, while the old cobbled streets round the citadel seem like a different world, one of traditionally dressed peasants living much the same as ever.

Given Ankara's background, it is fitting that the two major sights the city has to offer the visitor today should reflect its ancient and its modern ties: the Anadolu Medeniyetleri Müzesi (Museum of Anatolian Civilisations) and Anıt Kabir (Atatürk's Mausoleum).

Ankara is located 459km (285 miles) from Istanbul, 250km (155 miles) from Konya, 506km (314 miles) from Antalya and 433km (269 miles) from Samsun.

Anıt Kabir (Atatürk's Mausoleum)

Visitors to this tomb can see in tangible form the personality cult built around this remarkable man, who died in 1938 but whose picture still hangs in every private house and public place. The sheer scale of the monument is overwhelming: the area occupies an entire hill of beautifully kept gardens bristling with smartly uniformed guards. The colossal limestone building itself is a cross between a classical temple and a modern monument. The stone sarcophagus weighs 40,000kg (39 tons).

The monumental mausoleum dedicated to Kemal Atatürk in Ankara

Ankara

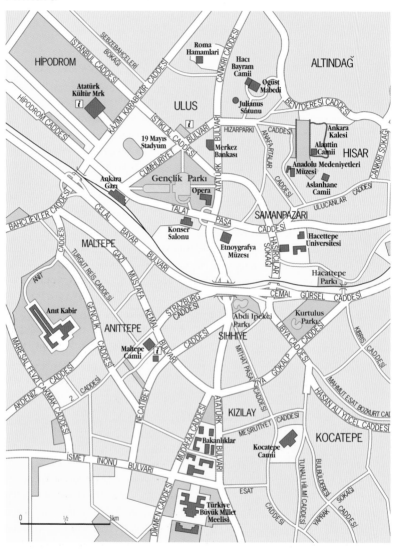

Anıt Caddesi. Open: daily, summer 9am–5pm; winter 9am–4pm. Sound & Light show in summer at 9pm. Free admission.

Ankara Kalesi (Citadel)

This is the oldest part of Ankara, with foundations dating back to the 3rd century BC. The defence walls visible today are Byzantine and Ottoman, and in the narrow streets within children still play barefoot in the dust, oblivious to the pace of change in the modern city below.

Anadolu Medeniyetleri Müzesi (Museum of Anatolian Civilisation)

Originally called the Hittite Museum, this small but carefully laid out museum is the most spectacular and comprehensive display of Hittite and Urartian finds in the world. The building itself is a renovated 15th-century Ottoman *bedestan* (covered market). In the central courtyard, the monumental stone Hittite carvings are displayed.

Do not miss the Anatolian earth mother, grotesquely fat by modern standards, with bulging arms, legs, breasts and belly. Female fatness was admired in Turkey until very recently. An Ottoman saying ran: 'She is so beautiful she has to go through the door sideways.'

Anafartalar Caddesi. Open: summer 8.30am–noon & 1.30–5.30pm, winter 8.30am–12.30pm & 1–5pm. Closed: Mon. Admission charge.

Roman Ankara

A handful of Roman monuments remain in Ankara, the principal ones being the Ogüst Mabedi (Temple of Augustus), the Julianus Sütunu (Column of Julian) and the Roma Hamamlari (Roman baths).

Off Çankırı Caddesi. Free admission.

Amasya

Amasya was the capital of the Pontic Empire, a small kingdom founded by a Greek tyrant. Today it is visited for its pretty river setting with timbered Ottoman houses overhanging the bank, and for the Pontic remains on the cliffside, Kızlar Sarayı (Maidens' Palace) and Kralkaya (King's Rock), the latter involving a steep ascent to the kings' tombs carved out of hard basalt. A few attractive Islamic buildings have also survived down in the town.

A ruined lunatic asylum, built in 1308 under the Mongol ruler Tamerlane, stands on Amasya's river front.

352km (219 miles) northeast of Ankara, 183km (114 miles) northeast of Boğazkale and 127km (79 miles) south of Samsun. The cliff sites are open: 8.30am–6pm.

Admission charge.

Hillside houses in Ankara

The Hittites

Until a century ago the Hittites were a mystery race mentioned only in the Old Testament (Uriah the Hittite) and in ancient Egyptian hieroglyphs.

Then in 1834 the first archaeological evidence of their existence was discovered at Boğazkale (Hattuşaş) in central Anatolia, and later excavations revealed thousands of cuneiform tablets which pieced together the history of the lost Hittite Empire.

The most remarkable thing about the Hittites is that, contemporary with the valley cultures of the ancient Egyptians and Babylonians, they were the only early civilisation to thrive in inhospitable mountain country. They were not indigenous but came in a great surge originally from southern Russia and central Asia. From their capital Hattusas they ruled Anatolia from the 19th to the 13th century BC. Practical and intellectually unpretentious, they devised a body of 200 laws covering every crime they could imagine. Murder, black magic and theft could all be compounded by

A lion stands guard by the Pyramidal Fire Altar

In Nemrut Daği, a well-known archaeological site, colossal Hittite sculptures litter the ground

a money payment or by restitution of property. The offences they singled out for capital punishment were defiance of the state, rape and sexual intercourse with animals. For currency they used silver bars or rings.

Their most enduring legacy today is their powerful rock sculpture, simple colossal representations of Hittite gods, especially their weather god Teshub, their sacred bull and lions guarding gateways.

The emergence of the Hittites from almost total obscurity has been one of the great achievements of archaeology during the 20th century. As most of the research into this civilisation has been reported by German and Czech scholars, it is not as famous in the English-speaking world as it deserves to be. It was in fact one of the greatest Bronze Age civilisations, speaking one of the earliest recorded of the Indo-European family of languages, the source of most of the languages of Europe and northern India.

The great arch has now collapsed, but the Lion Gate at Boğazkale is still guarded by its creatures

Boğazkale (Hattuşaş)

The Hittite capital of Boğazkale covers a vast area and to explore it on foot would take three or four hours. A car is advisable to reduce the effort of the long, steep, shadeless climb, especially in summer.

Boğazkale means 'fortress of the narrow mountain pass', and the site was chosen because of its naturally defensive topography and because of the unusual abundance, in central Anatolian terms, of fresh water. The defensive wall was 6½km (4 miles) long, with 200 towers.

Mostly you will see only foundations and low walls, but what impresses is the size and scale of all the buildings. At each of the three corners of the top plateau stand the three city gates, Lion Gate, Sphinx Gate and the King's Gate, all about 500m (550yds) apart.

Start with Lion Gate and notice the lion's characteristically Hittite carved mane, whiskers and hairy chest. The Sphinx Gate's sphinxes are now in museums but you can walk through the 70m (77yds) long postern tunnel, a remarkable piece of military engineering. King's Gate bears a copy of the original smiling war god now in the Ankara museum.

Lower down are the fortified royal palaces, and then the great temple of the weather god, the largest and best preserved of any Hittite temple, surrounded by 78 storerooms, some still with colossal storage jars for wine and oil.

206km (128 miles) east of Ankara, 181km (112 miles) southwest of Amasya. Open: daily 8.30am–6pm. Admission charge.

Boğazkale environs

Alacahöyük

This is a much more compact city than Boğazkale, and conveys more clearly the feel of a fortified Hittite town. You can walk along the main street with its Hittite drainage, admire the elaborate reliefs on the Sphinx Gate and discover the ingenious underground postern tunnel. There is a small museum on site.

36km (22 miles) north of Boğazkale. Open: daily 8.30am–noon & 1.30–5.30pm. Admission charge.

Yazılıkaya

This is the extraordinary 13th-century BC rock-cut open-air sanctuary of Hattuşaş, set in a group of rock clefts among pine trees, unique of its kind.

Detail from Sphinx Gate, Alacahöyük

Apart from Karatepe (*see p85*), it is the only Hittite site to have all its rock reliefs *in situ*.

3km (2 miles) east of Boğazkale. Open: daily 8.30am–6pm. Admission charge.

Konya

Konya is Turkey's most religious city, home of the mystic Sufi sect of Islam and its famous Whirling Dervishes. Their centre was the Mevlana Tekke, the heart of Konya, with its unforgettable blue-green dome, which remains the highlight of any visit today.

Besides the Mevlana Tekke, Konya also has a number of beautiful buildings dating from the 12th and 13th centuries when Konya served as capital for the Seljuks and was a haven of Muslim art and culture.

Konya lies 250km (155 miles) south of Ankara, 256km (159 miles) northwest of Silifke.

Mevlana Tekke (Monastery)

This sacred shrine and object of Muslim pilgrimage from all over Turkey is where Mevlana (*see pp126–7*) was buried in 1273. It is now a museum, but the atmosphere of reverence remains almost tangible.

It was round the fountain in the front courtyard that the dervishes whirled. The heavily decorated dervish tombs lie inside the main building, draped in richly embroidered cloths and with the distinctive turban on top. Mevlana's own is covered in his own poetry, and the blue-green dome rises directly above his tomb. The displayed treasures were all gifts from sultans and princes to the Mevlevi order.

Kışla Caddesi. Open: daily 9am–noon & 1.30–5.30pm. Admission charge.

Alaeddin Mosque

The largest mosque in Konya, it took 70 years to build. Eight Seljuk sultans are buried inside. It is set at the foot of the Alaeddin Park, the former acropolis in Roman times, where there are gardens and cafés. Completed in 1221, it is still a working mosque.

Alaeddin Bulvarı.

Karatay Medrese

Opposite the Alaeddin Mosque stands this theological college built in 1258, with a magnificently carved entrance portal. It is now a museum for Seljuk and Ottoman tiles. The interior domed ceiling is stunningly decorated with yellow stars against a deep blue background.

Alaeddin Bulvarı. Open: daily 9am–noon & 1.30–5.30pm. Admission charge.

Konya environs

Alahan Monastery

This remote ruined Byzantine monastery complex, built at the end of the 5th century in its magnificent mountain setting, should not be missed. Approaching visitors first see the great western basilica with elaborate relief sculptures of the archangels Gabriel and Michael trampling pagan gods underfoot. The eastern church was built about 50 years later, and is

Mevlana Tekke, Konya, is built around the mausoleum of the dervish order's founder, Rumi

beautifully preserved, with an appearance of grace and elegance. *161km (100 miles) southeast of Konya, 24km (15 miles) northwest of Mut. Open: daily 8.30am–sunset. Admission charge.*

Sivas

One of the Seljuk Empire's principal cities, Sivas is still adorned with beautiful Seljuk buildings. The most famous is the Çifte Minare Medrese (Twin Minaret Madrasa), prominent in the main square. Curiously, it is only a façade, the main structure having collapsed long ago. The other major monuments are the Gök Medrese, the Şihafiye and Buruciye Medrese, and the Ulu Camii with its leaning tower. *441km (274 miles) east of Ankara, 220km (137 miles) southeast of Amasya.*

Sivas environs
Divriği

The single reason for visiting Divriği (*see map pp4–5*) is the extraordinary 13th-century mosque-madrasa complex, a unique architectural phenomenon, almost reminiscent of something from the Indian Moghul Empire. *165km (103 miles) east of Sivas, 192km (119 miles) north of Malatya. Open: daily 8.30am–6pm. Free admission, but tip the guardian.*

Tokat

This central Anatolian town is famous for one monument, the

Gök Medrese in Sivas was built in 1271

Gök Medrese (Turquoise Madrasa), named after the colour of its tiles. Now a restored and prettily laid-out museum, the madrasa was built in 1275. *103km (64 miles) north of Sivas, 117km (73 miles) east of Amasya. Open: daily 9am–noon & 1.30–5.30pm. Admission charge.*

Tokat environs
Sulusaray (Sebastopolis)

This Roman city was only discovered in 1988, after a flood uncovered some of its marble columns. Its state of preservation promises to rival Ephesus, showpiece of the Aegean. Large sections of marble flooring and a gymnasium have been excavated so far, but it will be many years before the work is completed. *38km (24 miles) southwest of Tokat.*

Cappadocia

This unique region of volcanic landscapes and rock-carved churches was largely forgotten by the western world until rediscovered by a French priest, who published his vast research in the 1930s and 1940s. Its renown has now spread worldwide, and Cappadocia has become one of the most visited and photographed areas of Turkey.

The tourist season generally runs from April to November, but the place always looks lovely in the winter months when there is usually a coating of snow on the fairy chimneys. These chimneys

Cappadocia

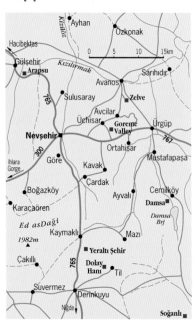

were formed by the effects of wind, snow and rain erosion over the course of millennia, on the soft porous volcanic rock called tufa. Unlike the harsh greys and blacks associated with most volcanic rock, the tufa has shades of yellow, pale grey, mauve, pink and umber, reflecting its mineral richness. The softness of the tufa lent itself to easy tunnelling, and various accidents of history meant that early Christians sought refuge from persecution here in cities they carved out underground. Over the 7th to the 14th centuries, monasticism flourished here, and hundreds of tiny churches were carved out of the rock, many of them containing fine paintings which have provided us with a remarkable record of religious art. What makes Cappadocia even more captivating is that it is still a living landscape, with numerous chimneys hollowed out for use as family homes or for storage.

Despite the tourist invasion, it is still possible to escape the madding crowd n the lesser-known valleys like Soğanlı nd Ihlara. The best range of ccommodation is to be found in Ürgüp, Avanos and Nevşehir. The sheer umber and variety of places to visit an be quite bewildering on a first visit. Here are some suggested day-trip estinations to help plan your stay.

Avanos

Avanos is a pretty town on the banks of he Kızılırmak (Red River), Anatolia's ongest. The distinctive deep red soil which colours the river water is much in vidence, and on a rainy day you will oon be covered in it. The red clay is still sed for the famous pottery, exported rom earliest times to Greece and Rome.

On the road south from Avanos to Ürgüp is the famous Peribacaları Valley of fairy chimneys with a forest of pinkish cones.

13km (8 miles) northwest of Ürgüp.

Derinkuyu

This amazing underground city was rediscovered in 1963. The full number of storeys that exist is thought to be as many as 18 or 20, but only the top 8 are open to the public.

In its heyday, some 20,000 people used to live here, and the advantages of this underground lifestyle were many. Apart from the obvious safety, temperature remained constant, there was year-round humidity and no insects. Air chimneys ensure excellent ventilation. The first two storeys contained communal kitchens, storage, stables, toilets, dining halls and bedrooms, while at the lower levels were hiding places with wells, churches, armouries, dungeons and graves.

53km (33 miles) southwest of Ürgüp, 30km (18½ miles) south of Nevşehir.
Open: daily 8am–6pm.
Admission charge.

he obelisk-like rock chimneys in the Göreme Valley

Göreme Valley

This open-air museum has now been designated a national park and is Cappadocia's major tourist attraction. There is no doubt that the churches within the valley contain the most spectacular paintings of the region, but there is a definite sense of being 'processed' through the site along roped-off walkways, following the arrows, which does detract to some extent from the enjoyment of the visit.

Göreme was one of the great centres of Christianity from the 6th to the 10th centuries and the Byzantine art on view here reflects a primitive provincial style, rich in colour and with an emotional intensity that was lacking in the formalism of contemporary work at Constantinople.

The paintings have been much damaged over the centuries by graffiti, mainly by the Byzantine Greeks themselves. They held that a brew of water and broken fresco fragments had miraculous healing powers, and the supplicant would carve his name and date beside the chunk he had chiselled out, to make sure God had registered who he was.

Most of the later defacement, literally, of Christ, Mary and the saints was carried out by local Muslim villagers for whom representation of the human form was a heresy, as only God could create this. Without faces, the figures were considered dead. *Göreme Valley is 11km (7 miles)* *southwest of Ürgüp. Open: daily 8.30am–6pm. Admission charge. There is also a car-park fee.*

Çarıklı Kilise (Church with the Shoes)

Reached by an iron staircase, the name comes from the shoeprints at the bottom of one of the pictures of Christ.

Elmalı Kilise (Apple Church)

An unusual 11th-century church, entered through a narrow tunnel, and with a dome over four pillars. There are fine frescoes of the Last Supper, the Betrayal by Judas and the Crucifixion.

Karanlık Kilise (Dark Church)

Part of a monastery complex whose façade has now fallen away, exposing the once dark interior, this church has colourful 11th-century frescoes of the Three Kings, the Last Supper and the Betrayal.

Kızlar Kilise (Convent)

This is a large complex on three levels with a refectory and kitchen, which once housed as many as 300 nuns.

St Barbara Kilise (St Barbara Church)

This has the plain red geometric lines of the Iconoclastic period (AD 726–843), when all representations of people in religious art were banned in the East. The red paint was made from the distinctive local clay.

Tokalı Kilise (Church with a Buckle)

Loveliest of the churches by far, the Tokalı lies outside the main ticketed area but is included in the museum ticket. It is by far the biggest of the Göreme churches, with magnificent frescoes set on an exquisite deep blue background. The colours and condition of the interior are still superb.

SYMBOLISM

The symbolic painting of the Iconoclastic period, when use of the human form was forbidden, meant that many symbols began to be used. Look out for the following:

cock	a white one is good luck, a black one is the Devil.
fish	the pious followers.
lion	victory and salvation.
palm	heaven and eternal life.
peacock	the resurrection of the body.
pigeon/dove	fertility, peace, love and innocence.
rabbit	sexuality, the Devil, magic.
vine	symbol of Jesus.

Yılanlı Kilise (Snake Church)

One of Göreme's most interesting churches, this has an arched ceiling and is famous for the remarkable painting of St George and the dragon, represented here as a snake, with the damned wrapped in its coils.

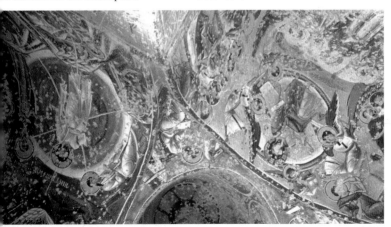

Frescoes in the Çarıklı Kilise, Göreme Valley

Drive: Around the Göreme

Though not a long drive, this 100km (62-mile) route cover
the numerous attractions around Göreme and will giv
you a feel of what greater Cappadocia has to offer. This i
definitely not 'off the beaten track' and you'll find yoursel
surrounded by hundreds of your fellow tourists, but if yo
enjoy this taster, you can wander off into the more remot
areas perhaps on foot or on horseback.

Allow 8 hours including stops.

1 Ürgüp

Start from Ürgüp, an atmospheric
amalgamation of rock-cut dwellings
and whitewashed traditional homes
tumbling down a hillside. One of the
most popular towns with a good tourist
infrastructure, the Sunday market is a
must for its handicrafts and carpets.
From Ürgüp head west on 767 route
to Nevşehir.

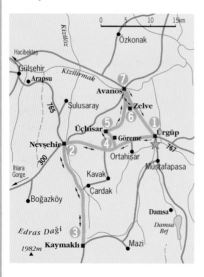

2 Nevşehir

Known in ancient times as Nissa,
Nevşehir is the largest town in the
Göreme region and is rather bland save
for the ruined Seljuk citadel that
crowns its peak. In the 1720s the town
was the birthplace of Grand Vizier
Damat Ibrahim Paşa, who endowed the
town with the Kurşunlu Camii (Lead
Domed Mosque) complex.
From Nevşehir travel south on route 765
to Kaymaklı.

3 Kaymaklı

This is the most accessible, though not
the biggest, underground city in the
area. Uncovered in the 1950s, it has
houses, kitchens, hospitals, wells, and
ventilation shafts over several storeys.
The underground dwellings are said to
be ancient – possibly Hittite – but were
developed to their current size (up to
20,000 inhabitants) during the latter
part of the first millennium as the
Christian communities hid from
marauding Arab raiders.

Retrace your steps from Kaymaklı to Nevşehir as if going back to Ürgüp. From the Nevşehir/Ürgüp road turn left to Göreme.

4 Göreme

The Göreme open-air museum (*see pp118–19*) protects some of the finest rock-cut churches in Cappadocia. Some date from the 4th century, though most are from the 10th and 11th centuries. Wandering the many lanes and footpaths that crisscross the valley, you'll find other churches along with 'chimneys' amongst small farmsteads and hectares of vines.

From Göreme head north to the tiny village of Üçhisar.

5 Üçhisar

The rock of Üçhisar, a vast crag honeycombed with man-made caves and rooms, stands guard over the collection of humble dwellings. This is the alter ego of the underground cities but still an impregnable fortress, and the more agile tourist can climb up inside for panoramic views across the countryside.

Head north again from Üçhisar towards Çavuşin and Avanos. The road leads through some typical Cappadocia landscapes. Stop and explore the Zelve Open-Air Museum.

6 Zelve

Where Göreme concentrates on its fine churches, Zelve has excellent natural features to admire as well as rock-cut churches and monasteries. Unfortunately, rock falls and erosion have made parts of the Zelve valley unsafe and sections will be off limits to the public.

From Zelve it's only a short drive to the small town of Avanos.

7 Avanos

Avanos is renowned for its pottery, created from the red earth that surrounds the town. It's a great place for souvenir shopping and has a collection of cafés for some welcome refreshment.

From Avanos take the main road south, 10km (6¼ miles) back to Ürgüp.

The ancient rock-cut churches in the Göreme Valley

Hacibektaş

Haci Bektaş was the founder of the Bektaşi Order in the 14th century, and Hacıbektaş is the name of the pretty monastery he established. It is now a museum, visited by many Turks as a holy shrine, and gives visitors an opportunity to see how a monastic community lived. The Bektaşi dervishes, or holy men, concerned themselves with the rural poor.

68km (42 miles) northwest of Ürgüp, 45km (28 miles) north of Nevşehir. Open: daily 8.30am–5.30pm. Admission charge.

Ihlara Gorge

See pp124–5.

Kaymaklil

Smaller than Derinkuyu, this underground city is known to be linked to it by a 9km (6-mile) long tunnel wide enough for four people to walk abreast. Discovered in 1964, it has a mere four storeys.

47km (29 miles) southwest of Ürgüp, 24km (15 miles) south of Nevşehir. Open: daily 8am–noon & 1–6pm. Admission charge.

Kayseri

The extinct volcano that created the Cappadocian landscapes, Erciyes Dağı (3,916m/12,848ft), rises behind this town, which is notorious for its merchants, especially carpet sellers, whose shrewdness is the subject of several Turkish proverbs. The Seljuk citadel, built of black basalt, is considered one of the finest extant examples of Seljuk military architecture. It now is a shopping precinct, as befits the local entrepreneurial spirit. Incongruously scattered about the town are several conical *kümbets* (tombs), dating from the 13th and 14th centuries.

328km (204 miles) southeast of Ankara, 87km (54 miles) east of Ürgüp.

Ortahisar

Visited for its huge honeycombed fortress which gives fine photographic opportunities over the landscape.

7km (4¼ miles) southwest of Ürgüp.

Özkonak

The largest of the Cappadocian underground cities, once housing 60,000 people, Özkonak is also the most recently discovered.

25km (15½ miles) north of Ürgüp. Open: daily 8.30am–6pm. Admission charge.

Niğde

A town built round an 11th-century citadel, Niğde boasts a few Seljuk and Mongol monuments of its own, but is visited chiefly for the monastery of Esk Gümüş, 14km (8½ miles) to the north off the Kayseri road. This is a very pretty monastery, unique in Cappadocia, with an open courtyard and rooms cut into the rock all around. The main church has delightful frescoes.

105km (65 miles) south of Ürgüp. Monastery open: daily 9am–noon & 1–5pm. Admission charge.

Fairy chimneys of Cappadocia

Soğanli

Taking its name from the pretty troglodyte village that sits above it, the Soğanlı valley divides into two forks, with signs indicating the location of the various churches. Of the 60 or so churches, the most interesting are Yılanlı Kilise (Snake Church), Saklı Kilise (Hidden Church), and the unusual three-storeyed Kubbeli Kilise (Domed Church) in its own weird rock formation. They are all in the right-hand valley fork.
47km (29 miles) south of Ürgüp. Open: 8.30am–5.30pm. Admission charge.

Sultanhani

This is the most colossal and best-preserved caravanserai in Turkey. Built in 1232 by the Seljuk sultan Keykubad I, the *han* provided the travelling merchant with somewhere to feed and water his animals, repair his vehicles, rest and recuperate himself and be fed, all free of charge and for up to three nights. Trade under the Seljuks flourished under such conditions. *48km (30 miles) west of Aksaray, 108km (67 miles) northeast of Konya.*

Üçhisar

Boasting a tall conical cone like Ortahisar, you can follow the signs to 'Kale' to climb to the top for the views. At night the cone is illuminated, looking like some Halloween gourd. *16km (10 miles) west of Ürgüp.*

Ürgüp

An attractive hilly rural town with cobbled streets in the heart of the main Cappadocian valleys, Ürgüp is the best base for excursions. It still has some old troglodyte houses of its own, in use as garages, storerooms or stables. Cappadocia's museum is located here, and there is good souvenir shopping along the main street.
Kayseri Caddesi, 87km (54 miles) west of Kayseri and 20km (12½ miles) east of Nevşehir. Museum open: Tue–Fri & Sun 8am–5pm. Admission charge.

Zelve

A pretty series of three valleys, dug out with cave dwellings, is now Zelve Open-Air Museum, making an attractive walk round various unusual buildings set in typical Cappadocian landscapes. The first valley has a rock-cut mosque, the only one of its kind, with a spectacular monastery complex cut out of a cliff-face. Churches and a rock-cut mill can be found in the second and third valleys. Zelve was occupied by a Turkish community until the 20th century.
19km (12 miles) northwest of Ürgüp, 6km (3¾ miles) south of Avanos. Open: daily 8.30am–6pm. Admission charge.

Walk: Ihlara Gorge

Lying slightly off the beaten track, this is a good trip to escape the crowds and explore a few early rock-cut churches set in magnificent gorge scenery. You need to be feeling fairly energetic for the steep descent into the gorge (formerly called the Peristrema Valley by the Greeks), taking about 10 minutes, with the ascent taking about double.

Allow a full half day, or an entire day if you want to do some extra walking.

To reach Ihlara from Nevşehir involves a scenic drive of 90 minutes southwest. After forking off the main Aksaray road at the yellow sign to Ihlara, the final 30km (19 miles) are along a narrow road dominated by the snow-covered volcano Hasan Dağı, 3,268m (10,722ft) high. You pass through a few semi-troglodyte villages, the last of which is Selime at the entrance to the gorge, where a conical tomb stands on the river bank.

The starting point of the walk lies just before Ihlara village, where you fork left and suddenly come upon a modern resthouse with superb terraces overlooking the gorge. It is open mid-May to mid-November, and offers good food and a handful of rooms for dedicated church explorers.

The Ihlara Gorge

From the resthouse you embark on the descent into the gorge down the specially built wide concrete steps.

There is a ticket office at the top where an admission charge must be paid (open: 8am–sunset).

The 150m- (490ft-) deep gorge was formed thousands of years ago by the erosion of the Melendiz river flowing north into Tuz Gölü (the Great Salt Lake). The river itself is the product of melting snow from Hasan Dağı.

Fresco in the Church with a Snake

The Ihlara Gorge, famous for its 6th-century Armenian refugee churches

The churches

The major churches in the gorge are signposted, and just before the bottom you come to the first church Ağaçlı Kilise (Church under a Tree). Carved out of the cliff face, it still has well-preserved frescoes, most notably of Daniel in the Lion's Den.

Turn right at the valley bottom to reach the Purenliseki Kilise (Church with a Terrace) which has fragmentary frescoes. Continuing along the path and around a jutting-out cliff where a colossal landslip has occurred, you come to the Kokar Kilise (Fragrant Church) with some attractive paintings outside.

Now retrace your path past the concrete steps to reach the Sümbüllü Kilise (Hyacinth Church), with arches and an elaborate façade carved into the rock. A few metres further on there is a wooden bridge which is crossed to reach the Yılanlı Kilise (Church with a Snake), where the sinners at the Last Judgement are portrayed wrapped in the coils of snakes.

Cross back over the bridge now to reach the other three main churches in the gorge, the Kırk Damlı Kilise (Church with Forty Roofs), the tiny Bahattın Samanlığı (Church with a Granary), and the Direkli Kilise (Columned Church) with three aisles and good paintings.

In the full 16km (10 miles) of the two sides of the gorge, there are over 100 rock-cut churches and several monasteries, and it is very pleasant to wander further afield in search of these if you have the time and energy. The only sounds accompanying you as you wander around exploring are the rushing river and the wind catching in the poplar trees. All around, the green fertile river banks are alive with an abundance of small creatures, birds, frogs, lizards and butterflies.

The Whirling Dervishes

The foundation of the Mevlana Order of Whirling Dervishes was the Seljuks' most important contribution to religion. Konya, capital of the old Seljuk empire, was where they were based. The 'whirling' is a unique form of religious observance requiring a great deal of practice and concentration, and as part of his reform programme to secularise Turkey, Atatürk banned the dance in 1925.

Today a small community of dervishes remains, removed from the mainstream of Muslim worship. The only time when they can be seen whirling is at the internationally famous Mevlana Festival held every year from 9 to 17 December. The festival commemorates the death, in 1273, of Celaleddin Rumi, known as Mevlana, who is buried in Konya.

A mystic poet and philosopher, Mevlana believed in ecstatic universal love, a state which he induced by whirling round and round for many hours at a time, accompanied by mystical music played on the *ney*, a reed flute. The dance symbolised the revolution of the spheres. The right hand was held up to receive a

Whirling Dervishes in full flow

lessing from above and the left hand eld down to dispense the blessing o the earth below. The dervishes dressed in long white gowns and wore tall felt cones on their heads, as they still do at the annual festival.

Mevlana's tomb under the dome of the Mevlana Tekke, Konya

Eastern Turkey and the Black Sea coast

Eastern Turkey remains for most people an unknown. Though a land border with Iraq creates current concern, the east is tantalisingly different from the rest of the country, with vast stretches of steppe-punctuated, snow-capped volcanic peaks and by some of Turkey's most fertile regions. It is also the part of Turkey least touched by the west, and a startling contrast to sophisticated Istanbul or the slightly 'racy' holiday coasts.

ANI

A visit to this eerie Armenian ghost town is an unforgettable experience. The contrast of the green fertile landscape with the scenes of devastation all around is a striking one. In the 10th century the city, grown wealthy from its position on an east–west caravan route, outshone anything in Europe, while only Constantinople, Cairo and Baghdad rivalled it in the east. Known as 'Ani of a hundred gates and a thousand churches', what remains today are the colossal walls and the shells of a few of its most robust churches. Earthquakes and Mongol raids in the 14th century destroyed Ani forever. At its height, the population was 200,000, nearly four times the current population of Kars.

The sweeping slopes of Mount Ararat dominate the landscape around

Eastern Turkey

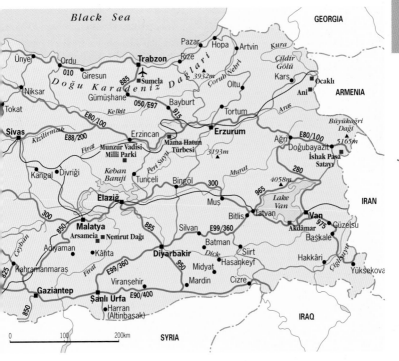

Black Sea

GEORGIA

Ünye · Ordu · Giresun · Trabzon · Pazar · Hopa · Artvin · Rize · Kura · Çıldır Gölü

010 · Sümela · Doğu Karadeniz Dağları · 3932m · Çoruh Nehri · Oltu · Kars · Ocaklı · Ani · ARMENIA

Niksar · Gümüşhane · 885 · Bayburt · 050/E97 · Tortum · Aras

Tokat · Kelkit · E80/100 · 915 · Erzincan · Mama Hatun Türbesi · Erzurum · Ağrı · E80/100 · Büyükağrı Dağı 5165m

Sivas · Kızılırmak · E88/200 · Fırat · Munzur Vadisi Milli Parki · 3193m · Doğubayazıt · İshak Paşa Satayı · 280

Kangal · Divriği · Keban Barajı · Tunceli · Bingöl · Peri Suyu · Murat · 300 · 4058m · 965 · IRAN

Elazığ · Muş · Lake Van · Van · 975 · Güzelsu

Malatya · Bitlis · Tatvan · Akdâmar · Başkale

Adıyaman · Arsameia · Nemrut Dağı · 885 · Silvan · E99/360 · Batman · Siirt · Hakkâri · Çığlıyayır · Yüksekova

Kâhta · Diyarbakır · Dicle · Midyat · Hasankeyf · Mardin · Cizre

Kahramanmaraş · Fırat · E99/360 · Viranşehir

Gaziantep · Şanlı Urfa · E90/400 · Harran (Altınbaşak) · IRAQ

825 · 850 · SYRIA

0 · 100 · 200km

Tour of Ani

Photography is now permitted on the site, and visitors are no longer given a soldier as an escort. The area inside the walls has been laid out in neat paths with signposts. The atmosphere is very silent, almost haunting, yet not in any way frightening. Away from cars and buses, shops and bustle, it is a tranquil experience.

The border between Turkey and Armenia/Georgia (formerly the USSR) is formed by the Arpa Cayı, a river set down in the ravine. The former USSR border posts are green and the Turkish posts grey.

Because of its location in the 700m (765yds) of no man's land between the Armenian and Turkish borders, you need a special permit to visit Ani. It takes half an hour to obtain this permit from the Kars Tourist Office (*open: 8.30am–12.30pm & 1.30–5.30pm*) and the *Jandarma* (police station), and visitors need passports and car documentation to fill in the forms. If you want to visit Ani the same day, do not arrive at the Tourist Office later than 2.30pm. Ani can only be reached by road, and the drive takes 40 minutes. Taxis can be arranged.
Ani lies 44km (27 miles) east of Kars.

Cathedral of Ani

The largest Armenian building still standing here or anywhere in Turkey, this late 10th-century church is superbly proportioned with most of its ceiling intact. Like most Armenian architecture, it has a very high ceiling in relation to its length and width. There are no murals, but the beauty lies in the graceful proportions and delicate blind arches.

Church of Gagik I

This church is unique in Armenian architecture in its circular groundplan. Built in 1001, the roundness made it an inherently weaker structure and it has not survived the earthquakes very well.

Menüçer Camii

This unusual mosque, built in 1072, stands on the edge of the ravine, and the inside feels more like a palace than a mosque.

St Gregory's Church

Labelled Resimli Kilise (Church with Pictures), this is the loveliest of Ani's remaining churches, built in 1215 with beautiful murals inside and out, painted on a deep royal blue. They depict scenes from the life of Gregory the Illuminator, Apostle to the Armenians.

Diyarbakır

This great old city, backed by the eastern Taurus mountains, sits on the navigable limit of the Tigris (Dicle) River. Its location means that it effectively dominates the expanse of the northern Mesopotamian plain.

Concentrated within its 5km (3-mile long black basalt walls, the city has the vibrance and vitality that comes naturally to a place that has been important for centuries, and still remains a key city of the southeast. Diyarbakır has more historical mosques, churches and other notable buildings than any other Turkish city except Istanbul.

Touring Diyarbakır's monuments, note the distinctive black-and-white striped effect, achieved by using the pale limestone with the black basalt, both found locally.

Diyarbakır is 188km (117 miles) northeast of Urfa, 548km (341 miles) northeast of Ankara & 402km (250 miles) southwest of Van.

The walls and the citadel

Of the original 72 towers that once surrounded this city all but five are still standing. You can still walk on a wide grassy path along the top of them between the Urfa and the Mardin Gates. Of the gates that led to the city, Harput Gate is the best preserved, but i is the Saray Kapı (Palace Gate), the one that leads into the citadel, that is the most beautiful.

The mosques and churches

Begin with the great 11th-century Ulu Cami, modelled on the Great Umayyad Mosque at Damascus. The loveliest of the rest are the Safa Mosque, the

Iskender Paşa and the Behrem Paşa. Also visit the Syrian Orthodox Church and the Armenian Surp Giragos Church, both of which are still in use.

Diyarbakır environs
Hasankeyf
This spectacularly sited ruined town sits on a cliff overlooking the Tigris. A 12th-century bridge spans the river, and you can walk up to the 12th-century ruins on the cliff top which cover over 2sq km (³/4 sq mile), complete with palace, mosques, tombs and private houses.
142km (88 miles) northeast of Mardin, 44km (27¹/2 miles) north of Midyat. Open: always. Free admission.

Mardin
Built up on a craggy rock overlooking the Syrian desert, this town is an important Syrian Christian centre with lovely Arab-influenced architecture, all concentrated in the citadel area. The Sultan Isa Medrese, built in 1385, is the best example, and there are fine views over the town from its roof. Mardin is sometimes called the 'White City', because of the pale stone used in the buildings, in contrast to black Diyarbakır.
96km (60 miles) southeast of Diyarbakır, 83km (52 miles) northwest of Nusaybin.

Tûr Abdin monasteries
In this fascinating pocket of land between Mardin, Midyat and Nusaybin, the Syrian Orthodox community flourished from the 5th century onwards. In medieval times there were four bishoprics and 80 monasteries here. Of these, four are still functioning with a handful of monks, and the remainder are ruined shells in use as cowsheds or grainstores. **Deyrulzaferan** (House of Saffron) is the most accessible monastery, 7km (4¹/4 miles) south of Mardin, with one monk and one nun remaining. Visitors can attend evening service at 6pm in Aramaic, the language of Christ.

Midyat is a curious town in two halves, the Christian half with its churches and bell towers, and the Muslim half 2km (1¹/4 miles) away. The most flourishing of the monasteries lies 20km (12¹/2 miles) east of Midyat, called **Mar Gabriel**, with six monks, ten nuns and a bishop. A monk will take you on a guided tour.

Doğubeyazit
This is a drab frontier town used as the base for the ascent of Büyükağrı Dağı (Mount Ararat, *see p146*). The town itself has little to offer the visitor, but people still come to see the famous and much photographed Ishak Pasha Saray, the Turkish Taj Mahal, which stands aloft on a hillside 6km (3³/4 miles) away to the south.
93km (58 miles) east of Ağri.

Ishak Pasha Saray
This remarkable pleasure palace was built around 1800 on the orders of Ishak Pasha, the local feudal chieftain.

The result is an extraordinary mixture of Seljuk, Persian, Georgian, Armenian and baroque Ottoman styles including stained-glass windows and every possible comfort. To ensure that the Armenian architect could not design a similar palace for a rival chieftain, his hands were ordered to be chopped off.

Much of the damage and blackening of the walls was caused by the Russian army in the Crimean War, when 400 soldiers slept in the harem rooms intended for Ishak Pasha's 14 concubines. *99km (62 miles) east of Ağri, 228km (142 miles) southeast of Kars & 328km (204 miles) north of Van. Open: daily 8am–4pm. Admission charge.*

Elazığ

A little-known place, Elazığ has a remarkable museum on the campus of the Euphrates University. It houses the items salvaged from archaeological digs before the creation of the Keban dam on the Euphrates resulted in the flooding of 50 early settlements. The collection of Urartian (*see p137*) objects on display – gold belts, ivories and jewellery is even more magnificent than that in the Ankara museum. Five kilometres (3 miles) to the north stands the derelict old fortress city of **Harput** with a 13th-century castle. The magnificent 14th-century castle of **Eski Pertek**, 24km (15 miles) to the north, is now inaccessible as the rocky outcrop it perches on is now surrounded on all sides by the new lake.

104km (65 miles) northeast of Malatya, 179km (111 miles) southeast of Divriği. Museum open: 9am–noon & 1.30–5.30pm. Admission charge.

The Ishak Pasha Palace displays a wonderful amalgamation of architectural influences

Erzincan

Destroyed many times by earthquakes, its very name means 'life crusher'. The important Urartian site of **Altıntepe** lies 16km (10 miles) to the east, where a wealth of gold and bronze was discovered in tombs untouched by grave robbers. On the hilltop are a well-preserved temple, a palace and a great hall.

190km (118 miles) west of Erzurum, 248km (154 miles) south of Trabzon.

Erzurum

Culturally something of a high point in eastern Turkey, boasting the main university, with strong archaeology and agriculture faculties, Erzurum has two famous monuments. The Yakutiye Medrese was built in 1310 by the Mongols, with pretty turquoise tiling on the minaret, and the Çifte Minare Medrese (Twin Minaretted Madrasa), built of brick in the 13th century by the Seljuks. Both monuments are in the centre of the old town near the main square and the Ulu Cami (Great Mosque). Both are kept locked and are visible only from the outside. Nearby are some Seljuk conical tombs (*kümbets*), and the old Byzantine citadel. The new museum on the modern outskirts displays Urartian metalwork and Ottoman jewellery and costumes.

219km (136 miles) southwest of Kars, 322km (200 miles) southeast of Trabzon. Open: 9am–noon & 1.30–5.30pm. Admission charge.

Inside the Ishak Pasha Palace

Nemrut Dağı

This is easily one of eastern Turkey's best-known sites, the weird colossal stone heads set on a remote mountaintop. Historically Nemrut Dağı has almost no significance. It is no more than a vast funeral monument to the ruler of a small local dynasty who suffered delusions of grandeur. But for all that, it is astonishing and unlike anything else in the world. The kingdom only extended from Adıyaman to Gaziantep, and was called Commagene, established in the 1st century BC. It lasted less than 200 years. Antiochus I, the king who created this sanctuary, depicts himself here surrounded by, and as an equal with, the gods and great kings, yet he chose

Hercules' head on the eastern terrace of Nemrut Dağı

such a remote setting on the summit of the 2,150m (7,045ft) Nemrut Dağı that it was not discovered until after World War II. The first rough road was built up to it in the 1960s. Before that, ascent was by donkey and took two days.

The road up leads past a fine Roman bridge over the river Cendere and then past Arsameia, the Commagene capital, where you can explore a cave and tunnel and the heavily ruined town in a lovely grassy hilltop setting.

The road ends a 10-minute walk from the summit, and the rocky path brings you out on to the eastern terrace with the five colossal figures of Apollo, Fortuna, Zeus, Antiochus and Hercules, their heads toppled by earthquakes. The man-made burial mound rises behind and you then walk round to the western terrace where the same five

statues face the sunset rather than the dawn (also see p111).

It is best to time your arrival for after midday so that morning mists have cleared. Dress warmly, as the summit is always chilly.

76km (47 miles) northeast of Adıyaman, 52km (32 miles) north of Kâhta, 217km (139 miles) west of Diyarbakır, 263km (163 miles) southeast of Malatya.

Nemrut Dağı environs
Harran
Harran is where the Bible tells us Abraham lived until he was 75. Visitors come to see the mud-brick beehive houses, thought to be largely unchanged since biblical times apart from the TV aerials. There is also a large, ruinous 11th-century fortress and great mosque.

45km (28 miles) south of Şanlı Urfa, 25km (16 miles) north of the Syrian border.

Şanlı Urfa (Urfa)

Named Edessa by Alexander the Great, this ancient city later became the earliest Christian centre in Mesopotamia. Today it is a sprawling dusty city of no beauty, but is visited for its biblical associations with Abraham and the **Halil er-Rahman mosque** with its lovely Pool of Abraham. Legend has it that Nimrod, King of Assyria, threw Abraham on a funeral pyre here in anger at Abraham's destruction of the idols in his temple. To save him, God created a lake to put out the fire. Abraham is a revered prophet for Muslims as well as Christians, which is why this has become a place of pilgrimage. The pool is alive with sacred carp which it is forbidden to kill. The area all around is pleasant for strolling, with attractive cafés set in gardens. Beyond the pool, concrete steps lead up to the Crusader citadel where two columns are known as the Throne of Nimrod.

149km (93 miles) east of Gaziantep on the E24, 192km (119 miles) west of Mardin.

Samsun

The biggest town and port on Turkey's Black Sea coast, its population, now 300,000, has doubled in the last ten years as a result of urban migration. For Black Sea scenery at its best, with the green hillsides of the tea plantations tumbling right down to the sea, you need to follow the coast road from Ordu (168km/104 miles east of Samsun) eastwards through Trabzon to Hopa near the Georgian border.

365km (227 miles) west of Trabzon.

Aleppo Gate of the ruined fortress at Harran

Black Sea coast

Sümela

This ruined monastery and Nemrut Dağı are probably the two most visited sites in eastern Turkey. Clinging Tibetan-like to a sheer rock face above steep and heavily wooded slopes, it is a stiff 30-minute climb from where the road ends to reach the monastery. Far from any habitation and often shrouded in mountain mists, it has a haunting quality despite the large number of visitors. After wet weather the zigzagging forest path gets very muddy, so choose appropriate footwear.

Behind its imposing 18th-century façade, the monastery is in ruins as a result of a fire in the last century. Founded in the 6th century, the last monks only left in 1923 when all Greeks in Turkey went back to Greece in an 'exchange of populations'. Though severely defaced and covered in graffiti, many of the remaining frescoes are still very fine, notably the Adam and Eve series.

48km (30 miles) south of Trabzon.
Open: daily 8am–5pm.
Admission charge.

Trabzon (Trebizond)

The days when fabled Trebizond lay like a 'green Eden' at the foot of the Pontic mountains, a little Constantinople on the Black Sea, are long past. That said, as long as you arrive with realistic expectations, Trabzon does offer some interest.

Its relics today are its churches, dating from the time when Trabzon was capital of a Byzantine dynasty called Comnene, which survived here some 250 years, the emperor's son Comnenus having fled Constantinople when it fell in the Fourth Crusade in 1204. Trabzon's most famous relic is the Aya Sofya Cathedral on the outskirts of town, now a museum. As in Istanbul, the Ottomans converted it to a mosque in the 15th century, whitewashing the walls, thus saving the frescoes. Other buildings to look for in the town centre are St Anna, St Andrew and the Fatih Camii in the citadel area. On the outskirts of town, in the Soguksu district, Atatürk's Summer House and museum are sites of pilgrimage for many Turks.

365km (227 miles) east of Samsun, 250km (155 miles) west of Artvin & 322km (200 miles) northwest of Erzurum. Aya Sofya Cathedral open: Tue–Sun 8.30am–noon & 1–5pm. Admission charge.

Van

The whole Van area (*see map on p129*) was closed to visitors before 1960. Today it is eastern Turkey's most forward-looking town, with a university and several training schools. It lies 4km (2¹/₂ miles) away from the lakeshore, and in the modern town itself the only place of interest to the visitor is the small but well-presented museum with a superb display of Urartian gold jewellery. Van served for 300 years as capital to the little-known Urartian empire, successors to the Hittites. They were accomplished builders, favouring long thin spurs for their fortress cities. There are over 30 such fortresses scattered over their empire, the largest being Van Kalesi and Çavuştepe. Urartian-worked gold, silver and bronze was exported westwards. Evidence suggests that ancient

Greeks and Etruscans copied from Urartian originals.

402km (250 miles) northeast of Diyarbakır and 147km (91 miles) east of Tatvan. Museum open: Tue–Sun 9am–noon & 1–5.30pm. Admission charge.

Van Kalesi (Van Castle)

On the lakeshore 4km (2¹/₂ miles) west of the modern town stands the extraordinary Rock of Van, the Urartian citadel. It is a freak outcrop 2km (1¹/₂ miles) long and 100m (330ft) high, with one of the largest Urartian fortresses, colossal 8th- and 9th-century BC rock-cut tombs of the Urartian

The Cathedral of the Holy Cross, Akdamar Island, Lake Van

kings and a temple, as well as some crumbling Ottoman buildings. In Ottoman times Van Castle was a military base and up to 3,000 Janissaries and soldiers lived here.

Down below, your eye will be drawn by further ruins. This is all that remains of the Ottoman city of Old Van which once had one of the largest populations in Anatolia, two-thirds of which was Armenian. Its total destruction by the Turks after World War I is still a subject of controversy.

Van environs
Akdamar Island
This tiny island on Lake Van plays host to the Church of the Holy Cross, a masterpiece of early Armenian art. Built in 915, it has some excellent carved reliefs depicting biblical scenes, notably that of Jonah and the Whale.

Çavuştepe
The second-largest Urartian citadel after Van Kalesi, Çavuştepe lies on the road to

Carved relief on the walls of the Church of the Holy Cross, Akdamar Island

A view of the mountains behind an Armenian church situated on an island of Lake Van

Eastern Turkey and the Black Sea coast

Hakkâri. Here you can explore a temple, and a royal palace, still impressive for the beautifully carved blocks.
Open: daily 8.30am–sunset.
Admission charge.

Güzelsu (Hoşap)

The best example of a Kurdish castle to be seen in Turkey today, Hoşap looks, with its crenellated battlements and turrets, as if it has been lifted straight from a fairy tale. In its heyday it is known to have had 360 rooms and two mosques.
48km (30 miles) east of Van on the Hakkâri road.
Open: daily 8.30am–sunset.
Admission charge.

Hakkâri

There are no specific monuments to visit in this extreme southeastern corner of Turkey, but the journey down here from Van is worthwhile for the magnificent scenery which begins at the Zab valley and the superb mountaineering in the peaks east of Hakkâri and south of Yüksekova.
204km (149 miles) south of Van.

Van Gölü (Lake Van)

Lake Van is the largest in Turkey, seven times bigger than Lake Geneva. It sits at a height of 1,750m (5,741ft), surrounded by several peaks over 3,000m (9,850ft), and its water is six times saltier than normal sea water.

Turkish wrestling

Yagli güres is indisputedly the ultimate Turkish sport. It is also known as grease wrestling because the bare-chested wrestlers cover themselves with oil

Although you can't fail to notice that Turks are soccer fanatics, the King of Turkish sports is *yaglı güres* or grease wrestling. Comprising contests of strength and strategy between individual unarmed opponents, wrestling is the embodiment of traditional codes and values still very much prized by this 'bullish' masculine society.

The most important competitions in the wrestling world are the Kırkpınar, at Edirne close to the border with Greece. Why the championships should be held here is the stuff of legend, attesting to the strength and purity of spirit of the Ottoman soldier/wrestlers. In the various versions two elements remain constant. Firstly that the combatants died here of exhaustion than admit defeat. Then that fresh water gushed from their burial site. Kırkpınar means 'forty springs'.

Although it's known as grease wrestling, it is olive oil that is poured onto the skin. This is thought to be because the oil acts as a mosquito repellent. The wrestlers are barefooted and bare chested but they wear weighted leather trousers (*kisbet*) made of buffalo hide. The best fighting breeches weigh 13kg (28½lbs). The victor is the man who either picks up his opponent so that both feet leave the ground, or who pins his opponent's back to the ground.

The winner is presented with the Kırkpınar gold belt and prize money of TL10 billion, but sponsorship can raise the overall kitty to much more than that. The current champion of the wrestling world is Ahmet Tasci, who has won a record number of championships since the Turkish Republic was founded in the 1920s.

The Kırkpınar contest is a big event held during the second week in July, but there are smaller contests around the country.

The heat of battle

Getting away from it all

The country offers some easy getaways from the regular crowded routes. There are over 1,000 thermal springs, some with spas offering theraputic treatment. There is good rambling terrain amongst the 'fairy chimneys' and vineyards of Cappadocia, and inland from the Turquoise Coast Lycia has some excellent hiking. Gradients are easy and only normal fitness is required. If this is still too energetic, the same routes can be travelled on horseback.

BOAT TRIPS

With over 8,000km (5,000 miles) of coastline, it's not surprising that trips on the water form an integral part of a trip to Turkey. There is ample opportunity to take short trips to neighbouring beaches from all the main resorts, often in a traditional wooden *gület* (*see p144*). Another option is to rent a private boat for the day, which is inexpensive compared with the Côte d'Azur in France or Costa del Sol in Spain, and set your own itinerary.

The Greek Islands

Often visible just off the Turkish coastline, the Aegean Islands were once part of the Ottoman Empire but were ceded to Greece at various times throughout the 20th century, principally after the two World Wars. They offer a fascinating contrast with Turkey, and each has its own particular charm and attractions, being holiday destinations in their own right. The short sea crossing makes them perfect day trips.

If you take a regular ferry, prices will be cheaper and you'll be able to plan your own day once at your destination. Boat trips will have a set itinerary and will be more expensive but often include lunch on board. Compare offers and prices before you book.

Chios

Chios town has a fine castle and archaeological museum. It's better to rent a car or agree on a rate with a taxi to tour the island's other attractions.

Mastic villages (*mastihohoria*) with exceptional villas built by the Genoese in the 14th and 15th centuries.

Pyrgi village with its distinctive walls decorated with black-and-white geometric patterns called *xysta*.

Nea Moni, one of the most beautiful Byzantine religious sites in the Aegean. The church has exceptional mosaics.
Day trips from Çeşme and Foça:
May–Oct.

Kos

An earthquake in Kos town in 1933 damaged the modern structures but revealed a Roman city lying just below ground level. Today it's possible to walk through the excavated Agora and along Roman roads which lie side by side with 21st-century thoroughfares – now home to one of the liveliest bar scenes in the Mediterranean.

Later the Knights of St John built a castle here to protect Mandraki harbour. Just as in Rhodes they were ousted by the Ottomans.

Hippocrates was said to have been born in Kos Town, and the enormous tree in the centre of town is often pointed out as the spot where he lectured to his students. Though verified as one of the oldest in Europe at 2,000 years, this ancient tree is still too young to have been growing during the era of the famed physician.

Day trips from Bodrum: May–Oct.

Lesvos

The third-largest Aegean island, Lesvos has a long culture especially in the arts. It was the birthplace of 5th-century BC poetess Sappho, and a fertile land renowned for its olive oil.

The capital Mytilini has long been a trade port, thriving during Ottoman times, a legacy of which are the fine 19th-century mansions around the town. The medieval castle is one of the largest in the Aegean, whilst the Lesvos Archaeological Museum is one of the best in Greece with some exceptional Roman mosaics.

Day trips from Ayvalık: May–Oct.

A tourist yacht sails down the Rhodes Town harbour

Rhodes

Ancient Rhodes was the home of the Colossus – one of the 'Seven Wonders of the World', a leviathan statue that collapsed into the sea after an earthquake. The five harbours of Rhodes town have ensured its wealth throughout the ages – even today it is one of the Mediterranean's most popular cruise-ship ports.

The astounding citadel of Old Rhodes, with its immense 4km (2¹/₂-mile) curtain walls, was built by the Knights of St John when they settled here after being ejected from the Holy Land by Muslim forces in 1309. Within the walls they built superb headquarters for each of the *langues* or different nationalities that made up the contingent of Knights, a Grand Palace for their leader or Grand Master, and a 'state-of-the-art' hospital that today houses the Archaeological Museum.

In 1522 Ottoman forces besieged the citadel, wresting it from the Knights and establishing a Muslim town. They stayed in control for 400 years.

Today the Ottoman town makes a startling contrast to the Knights district. A maze of cobbled alleyways constitutes the commercial section of the city, now replete with souvenir shops, restaurants and cafés.
Day trips from Marmaris: May–Oct.

Samos

Samos Town, or Vathi, has a very Greek atmosphere and a fine harbour-front promenade. The small town of Pithagorio is the site of the ancient capital during the reign of Polycrates, who came to power in 538 BC. The storyteller Aesop and mathematician Pythagoras were both part of his court. The town tumbles down the hill to a beautiful harbour, protected by a giant mole, built on the orders of Polycrates.
Day trips from Kuşadası: May–Oct.

Gület cruising

Gülets are the traditional motor yachts that have been built for generations from the red pine that grows in abundance all over Turkey's southern shore. This coastline is increasingly becoming associated with *gület* holidays, where visitors spend their 7 or 14 days cruising in leisurely fashion from bay to bay, dropping anchor for a swim here, exploring an ancient city ruin there. Most boats sleep 8 to 12 people, and the Turkish crew sees to all the catering and the route, so all you have to do is sit back and relax. Space is limited on board so minimalist packing is called for. Most cabins have a private toilet and shower with hot water provided by the on-board generator. The boats are very attractive, with a shaded area on deck, and many have CD players so you can bring your own music. Children under 12 are not accepted, except if the whole boat has been booked by one party. Marmaris,

TRIP REMINDER

Don't forget – for trips to the Greek Islands and Northern Cyprus you'll need to take your passport!

Bodrum, Fethiye, Kalkan and Kaş are the main centres, but there are many more small fishing villages to call off at along the way. Holidays combining seven days' *gület* cruising with seven days on shore are becoming very popular. On a 14-day cruise it is possible to motor all the way from Bodrum to Fethiye, and transport is then arranged to get you back to the airport. Your local **Turkish Tourist Office** can supply you with a list of the many tour operators who specialise in *gület* cruising.

From Istanbul

Boat trips from Istanbul make a perfect antidote to days trudging the fascinating but dusty streets of the old Sultanahmet. A trip along the Bosporus (*see pp56–7*) is an excellent way to get a water's-level view of how the city works, while a full day away to the tiny, traffic-free Adalar Islands (*see p50*) offers total relaxation and some excellent restaurants.

Northern Cyprus

Separated from the south following the Turkish invasion of the island in 1974 in reaction to a coup by the Greek-backed army, The Turkish Republic of Northern Cyprus has been somewhat of a backwater for the last 30 years. It is remarkably unspoilt and uncrowded, with several impressive Classical ancient sites and spectacular medieval citadels. Kyrenia (Girne), with its Crusader castle and atmospheric harbour, makes the perfect base from which to set out.

Passenger boats from Mersin and Alanya to Girne (Kyrenia): several times per week, all year. Crossings take five hours from Mersin, eight hours from Alanya. Car ferry from Taşacu to Gazimağusa (Famagusta): weekly, all year.

Gülets by a rocky coast beneath Mount Olympos

LAKES AND MOUNTAINS

To truly escape the crowds, especially during public holidays when the beach resorts tend to be packed to bursting, head inland to explore Turkey's vast hinterland and its magnificent mountains and lakes.

Bafa Gölü (Lake Bafa)

Created by the silting up of the Latmos River in antiquity, Bafa is a world apart from the coastline only an hour away. The modern farming village of Kapıkırı now sits amongst the remains of ancient Heraclea. Other ruins sit evocatively on small offshore islands that are accessible by boat.

Inland from Kuşadası.

Beyşehir

Good for swimming, this lake has several restaurants at its outlet where you can enjoy a relaxing lunch. If you want to sightsee, there is an interesting 13th-century mosque and *türbe* on the shoreline.

From the Isparta road you can reach the enigmatic Hittite sanctuary of **Elflatunpınarı** with carved reliefs, now underwater.

North of Antalya.

Büyükağrı Dağı (Mount Ararat)

At 5,165m (16,946ft) Ararat is Turkey's highest mountain and its peak is snow-capped even in the height of summer. The usual route to the summit takes three days from Doğubeyazıt. The

ORGANISED TREKKING AND MOUNTAINEERING

Usually involving groups of 10 to 15, these are becoming increasingly popular. Mount Ararat and the Kackar range in the eastern half of the country present a serious challenge to stamina (though trekking here does not require previous experience). The Tauras mountains of Lycia in the west are more like hilly country walking. Your local Tourist Office will supply you with a list of the tour operators who specialise in these holidays. Baggage and supplies are usually strapped onto donkeys. Accommodation is a mix of hotels and camps.

descent takes one day and it is not considered a technical climb.

Eğridir

A green oasis amidst the Anatolian plateau, with the pretty town of the same name offering a Seljuk castle and old Ottoman houses to explore.

North of Antalya.

Kaçkar

Also known as the 'little Caucasus', this mountain range with steep, rocky peaks lies inland from the Black Sea. Starting point for the climbs is Çamlıhemşin, where the route leads up through high *yaylas* or summer pastures to peaks around 3,500m (11,500ft).

Lake Van

Lake Van's high alkalinity is caused by evaporation. Local fishermen keep their clothing 'whiter than white' by dangling it over the side as they hang their nets. It is also said to be therapeutic for the skin and is so alkaline that people float.

Tuz Gölü (Great Salt Lake)

Remarkable for its size, this shimmering expanse and the surrounding landscape are devoid of life but the shoreline is fascinating. *Southeast of Ankara.*

FLORA AND FAUNA

The national parks have allowed Turkey's rich flora and fauna to flourish in a protected environment, but many colourful flowers also grow wild on the hillsides and even on the roadsides in the Aegean and Mediterranean regions. April and May are the most impressive months, when the pink oleander bushes, red anemones and poppies, and white irises abound. Tumbling white jasmine and purple bougainvillea continue to bloom throughout the summer in many gardens.

In the western regions, the main form of wildlife encountered is the mosquito, though they are no worse

A stork looks out from its nest

here than in any other Mediterranean country. From April until September many types of butterfly can be found feeding on the flowers, but the rarer species like the white admiral and purple emperor are to be found inland. Scorpions and snakes are not abundant but do exist, so it is worth being careful if walking on rougher ground with bare ankles and legs. In the Aegean coastal areas it is common to see tortoises strolling across the quieter roads.

Along the roadsides on the southern Mediterranean, large, hairy, two-humped camels are still to be seen, giving way in Central Anatolia to the huge, black water buffalo, with their long beards and fierce horns. Both are used as beasts of burden. Sheep, goats and cattle are plentiful. In the remoter, more mountainous areas to the east, bears, badgers, boar, deer, ibex, jackals and gazelles can be seen, together with wild cats, wolves, wild dogs and even leopards in the forests.

Bird-watching

Armed with a pair of binoculars and a field guide (such as *The Birds of Britain and Europe with North Africa and the Middle East* by Heinzel, Fitter and Parslow), you can add a whole new dimension to your holiday. While there are specialist tour operators who offer bird-watching holidays, you can combine bird-watching with your own sightseeing or even with lazing on the beach.

Turkey offers a remarkably wide range of bird life due to its geographical position on the edge of Europe, Asia and Africa. Birds from all three continents are to be found here, and the unusually wide range of climatic conditions adds to the diversity. In spring and summer there is the added attraction of two major north–south migration routes. These migrations are on a huge scale: nearly 400,000 birds of prey have been recorded passing the northwest Black Sea coast in one season.

May is probably the best bird-watching month, and on a typical two- to three-week touring holiday, the profusion of bird life is such that even inexperienced bird-watchers can be assured of spotting well over 100 species. The large, distinctive birds that are so difficult to miss are the tall storks. Their enormous nests are often to be seen on minarets, rooftops and telegraph poles. Around rivers and lakes grey herons are also seen in abundance. Overhead, the wide-spread wings catching the thermals, vultures and birds of prey are common, if not always readily identifiable, and the bird that is always running off the tarmac and flying up under the wheels is the crested lark.

Turkey boasts several bird sanctuaries, notably Kuş Cenneti in Marmara, and at Birecik on the Syrian border, where the bald ibis, a large and extraordinary bird on the verge of extinction, is the subject of a World Wildlife Rescue Operation.

For more information contact **The Ornithological Society of the Middle East**, c/o The Lodge, Sandy, Bedfordshire SG19 2DL, England.

NATIONAL PARKS

Turkey is a country blessed with huge tracts of virgin landscape, and these have been preserved in recent years by the creation of many national parks. All are in heavily forested areas, often with lakes and rivers, and are rich in flora and wildlife. They are all open to the public and are free of charge.

Aegean region
Kuş Cenneti Milli Parkı (Bird Paradise)
A bird sanctuary situated just inland from the Sea of Marmara.
60km (37 miles) west of Bursa.

Sipildağı Milli Parkı
A national park where one can see the famous 'crying rock' of Niobe.
20km (12½ miles) northeast of Izmir on the Manisa Rd.

Uludağ Milli Parkı
A heavily forested area round Uludağ, the ancient Mount Olympos. In winter it is a busy ski resort, but in summer it is rich with lovely mountain walks amid streams and wild flowers (*see p51 & 161*).
35km (21½ miles) east of Bursa.

Mediterranean region
Beydağlari Olimpos Milli Parkı
This incorporates the ancient ruins of Olympos, and lies just inland from Kemer (*see p102*).
20km (12½ miles) south of Antalya.

Güllükdağı Milli Parkı

This is the park around the ancient city of Termessos high in the mountains (*see p89*).

34km (21 miles) northwest of Antalya, off the E24 towards Korkuteli.

Kızıldağ Milli Parkı

A beautiful park of cedar trees situated on the northwestern fringe of Lake Beyşehir.

North of Antalya.

Kovada Gölü Milli Parkı

Centred on a lake in the mountains.

25km (15¹/₂ miles) south of Lake Eğridir, inland from Antalya.

Köprülü Kanyon Milli Parkı

On the way to the ruins of Selge.

60km (37 miles) north of Side (see p103).

Central region

Boğazkale-Alacahöyük Milli Parkı

This incorporates the ancient Hittite sites of Boğazkale and Alacahöyük.

East of Ankara.

A Milli Parkı signpost in the Menderes valley

Çamlık Milli Parkı

Famous for its king eagles, this park is adjacent to Yozgat.

40km (25 miles) south of Boğazkale.

Göreme Milli Parkı

The beautiful Göreme valley and its rock-cut churches in Cappadocia.

Eastern region and the Black Sea

Altındere Milli Parkı

This incorporates the Sumela monastery.

45km (28 miles) inland from Trabzon on the Black Sea coast.

Ilgaz Milli Parkı

45km (28 miles) south of Kastamonu, inland from Inebolu on the Black Sea.

Karatepe Milli Parkı

The park is situated on the Cayhan River valley in Adana province and incorporates the ancient Hittite site of Karatepe.

100km (62 miles) northeast of Adana.

Munzur Vadisi Milli Parkı

One of the wildest areas of Turkey, where bears are still found.

50km (31 miles) south of Erzincan, near Ovacık.

Nemrut Dağı Milli Parkı

This incorporates the famous mountaintop heads on Nemrut Dağı.

60km (37 miles) south of Malatya.

Soğuksu Milli Parkı

110km (68 miles) inland from Zonguldak on the Black Sea coast.

Yedigöller Milli Parkı

Magnificent scenery with seven lakes, excellent trekking terrain.

50km (31 miles) inland from Zonguldak on the Black Sea coast.

Shopping

Turkey offers an unusually large variety of souvenirs, and most people are pleasantly surprised by the high standard and good value. In the bazaars, bargaining is the norm, and even when prices are marked, you should aim to knock around one-third off the first quoted price. As a general rule the longer you are prepared to spend bargaining, the better the deal you get. In shops like pharmacies, grocers, clothes boutiques, and so on, the prices are fixed, so there is no point trying to bargain over a packet of aspirin.

Normal shopping hours are 9.30am–1pm and 2–7pm; closed Sundays. The Covered Bazaar is open 8.30am–7pm; closed Sundays.

ISTANBUL

Istanbul is the shopping high point in Turkey, and nobody should miss the Covered Bazaar (*see pp52–3*), where virtually every souvenir can be found under the same roof. An annual Shopping Fest is held between February and March.

The Covered Bazaar

An exhaustive list is not possible, but among the main items you will find in the Bazaar are:

Alabaster: a translucent calcite or gypsum, made into chess sets, egg cups, ashtrays and so on.

Antiques: many are genuine but even more are fake. Export of antiques is strictly forbidden and carries a stiff prison sentence. If you buy something old, get the shopowner to state the age on the invoice and make sure he signs it.

Camel-bone boxes: beautifully painted.

Carpets: an apparently infinite selection of carpets and *kilims* at good prices (*see pp80–81*).

Ceramics: colourful abstract and floral designs on Islamic motifs, usually in blues and greens, made into jugs, pots, plates, bowls and tiles.

Copper and brassware: a brass tea tray with carrying handle and tea glasses makes an unusual and usable souvenir. Copper is toxic, so should not be used for eating and drinking vessels unless coated with tin on the inside, something which can be easily done in the market.

Denim: vast quantities of all kinds of denim clothing, and also cheap canvas bags in all sizes to carry home your purchases.

Gold and silver: the daily gold price is chalked up on a blackboard on Kuyumcular Caddesi, the Street of the Jewellers. The silver *han* (Kalcılar Hanı) has an amazing variety, and pieces can be made to order here in just a few days.

Jewellery: an extraordinary selection, often using semi-precious stones such as turquoise, amethyst, garnet, onyx, jade and lapis lazuli.

Leather and suede: all different shapes and sizes of coats, jackets, skirts, trousers, shoes, bags and belts. The leather is beautifully soft, but any purchase needs to be carefully inspected to check workmanship and exact sizing.

Spices: the whole range from ginger to curry, sold from open sacks; also at the Spice Market (Mısır Çarşışı) beside Yeni Camii, Eminönü.

Turkish delight: known as *lokum*,

HOW TO BUY A CARPET

1 Stick to Turkish pieces. While Iranian, Caucasian and Turcoman are available, they are often more expensive in Turkey than elsewhere due to rarity value.
2 Check closeness of weave by looking at the back. The closer the weave, the smaller the knot, the higher the price. Wet a handkerchief and rub it over to check colour fastness, and look carefully for repairs.
3 To check silk is not synthetic, put a match to the fringe. Real silk does not flame easily, while the synthetic glows and has a chemical smell. (*See also pp80–81.*)

which comes in flavours like lemon, mint or pistachio, packed and presented in every conceivable variety and quantity.

A taste of the exotic Orient – bejewelled dresses, popular with entertainers

Special interest shopping centres
Arasta Bazaar
Behind the Blue Mosque, Sultanahmet, a street of souvenir shops converted from the Ottoman sultan's stables, selling carpets, *kilims*, jewellery and brassware, at prices a little higher than the Covered Bazaar.

Beyazıt Sahaflar Çarşışı
The book market between the Covered Bazaar and the Beyazıt Mosque, excellent for all books new and old in all languages. Also good for calendars and Turkish miniatures.

Istanbul Handicrafts Centre
Beside the Yeşil Ev Hotel, Sultanahmet, where you can watch artisans at work and buy their creations.

Food and clothing
For fashion clothing, **Beymen** is the top-quality chain of Turkish-made men's and women's wear. A new children's range has also been launched. Ask your hotel reception for the nearest branch. **Benetton** and **Lacoste** also have shops here.

For food, the famous places are the **Fish Market** (Balıkpazarı) on Istiklal Caddesi, Galatasaray, Beyoğlu, and the **Egyptian Spice Bazaar** (Mısır Çarşışı) for spices, sweets and Turkish delight. **Migros** in Şişli district is the biggest supermarket, and **Printemps** at the Galleria Ataköy shopping mall, on the airport road, is the best department store.

The larger hotels in Istanbul, and indeed throughout Turkey, have their own souvenir shops, often with very high-quality goods, if somewhat expensive, but nevertheless very convenient for those short of time.

Istanbul environs
Bursa has a covered bazaar (*bedestan*) in the town centre, where the best buys are towels, knives and silk.

AEGEAN REGION
Bodrum
The main bazaar area is round the foot of the castle with shops selling wide selections of rugs, embroidery, copperware, sponges and lapis lazuli beads to ward off the 'evil eye'. Leisure clothes made of soft cotton also make a very attractive buy.
Dalyan
Has a small range of souvenir shops in the town.
Kuşadası
Has a large and lively bazaar offering the full range of souvenirs.
Izmir
Has a covered market just inland from the clock tower on the seafront.
Marmaris
The best shopping is in the renovated Ottoman caravanserai (Kervanseray).

MEDITERRANEAN REGION
The big cities of **Adana**, **Antalya** and **Antakya** all have covered bazaars in their centres. **Fethiye** has a bustling daily food market and lots of souvenir shops.

The resort villages of **Kalkan**, **Kaş**, **Kemer** and **Side** offer a sophisticated range of souvenir shops, including carpets and *kilim* shops, with lots of small, bright shops clustered in narrow streets.

CENTRAL REGION

Ankara

Copper, jewellery, carpets, costumes, embroidery and antiques can be found in the old shops in Çıkrıkçılar Yokuşu near Ulus.

Kayseri

A noted centre of the carpet trade, where many souvenir and jewellery shops now exist in the renovated citadel and bazaar areas.

Konya

Well known for its carpets. The souvenir shops are all in the centre, clustered near the Mevlana Tekke.

Ürgüp

This Cappadocian town has an excellent range of shops on its main street opposite the museum, selling silver jewellery, locally quarried onyx and nomad knitwear. Cappadocia is generally well provided with souvenir shops. **Avanos** is famous for its red pottery, made from the local red clay.

EASTERN TURKEY AND THE BLACK SEA

Souvenir shops are few and far between in eastern Turkey and on the Black Sea coast. Among the best buys available are carpets, nomad multicoloured knitted gloves and socks, and embroidered headscarves. In **Erzurum** the local black jet (*oltu*) is made into various artefacts such as worry beads and necklaces, on sale in the vicinity of the Ulu Camii.

Plenty of Turkish bric-a-brac to carry home as souvenirs

Entertainment

Throughout Turkey, the most commonly indulged form
entertainment is eating out or drinking tea and coffee
bars and cafés, watching the world go by, or playin
backgammon. Istanbul has the lion's share of the country
organised entertainment. Elsewhere there is little excep
discos in the resorts, and all cultural activity is concentrate
on the annual festivals such as the Bodrum Culture an
Art Week and the Antalya Film and Art Festival.

Cinema and theatre are currently undergoing a revival, especially in Istanbul, and the Atatürk Cultural Centres in Istanbul, Ankara and Izmir, Turkey's three main cities, offer classical music, ballet and operatic performances.

There are nightclubs presenting special shows with belly dancing and folk dancing, where the clientele is almost exclusively non-Turkish. Traditional Turkish dance and music are to be found in the annual festivals such as the Istanbul International Art and Culture Festival in June and July (*see p18*).

Discos are ubiquitous and usually good. Large city hotels sometimes have casinos and discos, all have bars and all have TV and in-house video. Turkish TV has a number of English shows and films, and the week's programmes are listed in the *Turkish Daily News*, Turkey's only English-language daily paper.

Listings for cinema and theatre are occasionally given in the paper, but more often you will have to ask or look out for adverts and posters.

ISTANBUL
Bars and cafés
All the major hotels have bars and cafés where non-residents are welcome The 'Street of Bars' in Kadiköy is very lively at night.

Les Ambassadeurs
A piano bar with luxurious atmosphere and fabulous Bosporus views.
Swissôtel, Maçka. Tel: 259 0101.
Open: 3pm–1.30am.

Bebek Bar
In the leafy residential area of Bebek, with a terrace overlooking the sea. Try the white cheese.
Cevdet Paşa Caddesi 15, Bebek.
Tel: 263 3000. Open: 7pm–1am.

Beyaz Köşk (White Pavilion)
In the grounds of the charming Emirgan Park in a restored 17th-century building, serving cakes, sandwiches and drinks.
Emirgan. Tel: 277 7061.

Çadır Köşku
et in the lovely Yıldız Park.
Yıldız Park, Beşiktaş. Tel: 260 0709.
Open: 9am–6pm.

Café Saray
In the magnificently restored Çırağan
Palace with a lovely summer terrace
overlooking the Bosporus.
Çırağan Palace Hotel Kempinksi,
Çırağan. Tel: 258 3377.

Cheers
In the heart of the old city, Cheers is a
popular young hangout with pavement
eating and serves a good selection of
salads and sandwiches.
Akbiyik Caddesi 20, Sultanahmet.

Country Life Café
This traditional-style Anatolian café
offers *narghiles* (hookah or shisha
pipes) and Turkish snacks served on
ow tables, and you sit on huge
cushions on the floor.
Dulcinea Poyraçık Sokak, Nişantaşı.

Dulcinea
Art gallery cum café with a good wine
ist and continental menu. There's also
regular live music.
Istiklal Caddesi, Meselık Sokak 20.
Tel: 245 1071.

Han Café
One of the trendiest places to be seen
in the early evening.
Cumhüriyet Caddesi, Taksim Sq.

Myott Café
The in-place for local yuppies, also
popular with foreigners for wholesome
breakfasts of muesli and fresh fruit.
Music. Iskele Sokak 14, Ortaköy.
Open: 9am–4pm.

Orient Bar
The bar and café of the well-known
Pera Palas Hotel.
Tepebaşı. Tel: 251 4560.
Open: 10.30pm–2am.

Tonoz Bar
In the restored Sepetçiler Palace, now
converted to an international press
centre. Peaceful, with good views.
Sepetçiler Kasrı, Kennedy Caddesi,
Sarayburnu. Tel: 511 4503.
Open: 8.30am–1am.

Casinos
There are casinos at around
15 Istanbul hotels.

Cinemas
Foreign films with Turkish subtitles are
mostly on Istiklal Caddesi in Beyoğlu.
They are Atlas, Beyoğlu, Dünya, Emek,
Fitas, Lale and Cinepop. Always double-
check programmes and timings.

Floor shows and revues
Galata Tower Restaurant
Belly dancing.
Karaköy. Tel: 245 1160.
Kervanseray
Belly dancing. *Elmadağ. Tel: 247 1630.*
Orient House
Belly dancing and Turkish folk dancing.
Beyazıt. Tel: 517 6163.
Parisienne
Belly dancing, disco and bar.
Elmadağ. Tel: 247 6362.
Regine Revue
Belly dancing and floor show.
Elmadağ. Tel: 246 7449.

A traditional musician in a Turkish café

Jazz clubs

Harry's Jazz Bar
Hosts occasional rock and blues bands.
Hyatt Regency Hotel. Tel: 225 7000.

Gramafon
The city's most enduring jazz venue.
Meydani 3, Tünel. Tel: 293 0768.

Q Jazz Club
Up-market; open-air venue in summer.
Çirağan Palace Hotel. Tel: 258 3377.

Music

The **Istanbul International Art and Culture Festival** (June & July) includes jazz, ballet and orchestral music as well as traditional Turkish music.

Istanbul Symphony Orchestra
Performs at the Atatürk Cultural Centre, the state's showpiece for classical music, ballet, opera and theatre.
Taksim. Tel: 251 5600.
Entry to rehearsals on Fri from 10.30am–1.30pm is free.

Nightclubs

Istanbul has a sophisticated 'clubbing' scene with some excellent open-air venues in summer. Cover charge and dress codes apply at all the top spots.

Babylon
One of the longest-running nightclubs in Istanbul, but it closes at midnight so you can make your way to another.
Seyhbender Sokak 3, Tünel.
Tel: (212) 292 7368.
Open: 10pm–4am.

Club 14
Young crowd with the latest sounds.
Abdulhakamit Caddesi, Belediye Dukkanlari 14, Taksim.
Tel: (212) 256 2121.

Joy Ortakoy
Focus on acid, jazz and Latin music.
Muallim Naci Caddesi Sokak 5 Ortakoy.
Tel: (212) 327 2844.

Hammam
A New Age restaurant. Transforms itself into a nightclub early morning.
Seoetciler Kary Sarayurnu.
Tel: (212) 511 6316.

Havana
Leading open-air venue.
Muallim Naci Caddesi 120 (in summer) Büyükdere Caddesi, Esentepe (rest of the year). Tel: (212) 213 0136.

Laila
Open-air dance floor. Bars nearby.
Muallim Naci Caddesi 141/2.
Tel: (212) 227 1711.

Soho
A supper club with resident DJs.
Mepekli Sokak 11/12, Taksim.
Tel: (212) 279 8699.

Theatres

Plays are sometimes performed in English. See listings in the *Turkish Daily News*.

Miscellaneous entertainment

AEGEAN REGION

Bodrum

Veli is a 'live blues' bar on Dr Alim Bey Caddesi. Other popular bars with music are **Greenhouse**, **Hadıgar** and **Kedıgarı**. **Disco Halikarnas** on Cumhuriyet Caddesi is probably the largest open-air disco in Europe.

Izmir

Surprisingly limited. There is the **Atatürk Cultural Centre** and the **State Ballet** (*Milli Kütüphane Caddesi; open late Sept–May*).

The **Izmir International Festival** runs mid-June to mid-July, but most events are actually held either in Çeşme castle or the Roman theatre at Ephesus. Programme and tickets available at the Opera and Ballet box office, the Çeşme Tourist Office or the museum in Selçuk.

Kuşadası

For the early evening head to **Barler Sokak**, 'the street of the bars'. Follow the crowd for hot spots.

Marmaris

Maxim's Disco
Kordon. Open: until 4am.

Palm Tree
Like a garden pub with taped music. Haci Mustafa Sokak 97.

MEDITERRANEAN REGION

Antalya

Nightlife centres around the yacht harbour. Two popular hotel discos are the **Olympos** (Falez Hotel) and **Disco X** (Hotel Kaplan).

Fethiye

Car Cemetery Bar features classic 60s–90s pop. Seating taken from old cars.

Kaş

The best bar is **Odeon Café Bar**, with **Nokta Redpoint** nightclub behind it.

Side

The best places in the old town are **Angels Café Bar** in the early evening, followed by **Lighthouse Disco** or **Oxyd**.

ANKARA AND CENTRAL REGION

Ankara

Ankara's best nightclub is the **Geceyarisi** (Cinnan Caddesi No 5-A; *tel: 426 1528*).
Also here are **The State Symphony Orchestra** and **State Opera and Ballet**.

Avanos

Dragon is the best nightclub in the region, with the best belly dancers. **Motif Restaurant** boasts a good folk-dancing programme (*tel: (4861) 1577*).

Ürgüp

Prokopi Pub-Bar and the **Karakuş Entertainment Centre**.

Children

The Turkish coast has all the raw material for keeping children happy. An abundance of sunshine, fantastic beaches and warm seas means low-key fun. Turks also love children. They always engage them quite spontaneously and are indulgent of boisterous behaviour in such places as restaurants. At mosque entrances they will help with children's shoelaces and carry pushchairs up steps without needing to be asked. That said, there are few specific attractions specifically designed for children. Here are a few suggestions.

Children love mosques. There is lots of space in the courtyard, with ablution fountains to chase round, windows to peep out of and sills to climb upon. Best of all, there is no pressure to be sober and pious.

Most children will love a holiday in any of the Aegean and Mediterranean resorts, with good beaches and pedestrian town centres. **Side** is probably the most suitable of all. Eastern Turkey is

less suitable as distances are large and long periods are spent travelling.

Istanbul

The whole of Istanbul is like one big playground, with mosques and palaces and museums to frolic in and large areas of green space (*see pp44–5*).

There are scores of actual playgrounds all over the city, notably along the European shore of the

There are many beaches in Turkey where children can play safely

Golden Horn and round the **Sea of Marmara shore**. Slides are huge with 40° slopes and amazingly steep seesaws. Safety consciousness is not much in evidence in Turkey. There are no cushioned landing areas in playgrounds for instance.

A permanent funfair with big wheel is set up on the shores of the Sea of Marmara on **Kennedy Caddesi**. At Ataköy, near the airport, there is **Fame City**, an amusements centre in the Galleria Shopping Mall.

The boat journeys up the Bosporus or to Princes' Islands are fine, but with small children it is best to avoid the public steamers because of the scrum in getting on and off, and the dirt. These steamers are also totally unsuited to pushchairs.

Children love the horse and carriage rides on Princes' Islands.

Beaches

The best beaches for young children, with safe sandy bays, are at **Alanya**, **Altınkum**, **Çeşme**, **Içmeler**, **Kemer**, **Ölü Deniz**, **Patara** and **Side**. Avoid the rocky beaches of Kaş and Kalkan and the Black Sea beaches near Istanbul, where there are very dangerous undertows.

Caves

At Burdur the **Insuyu Caves** are directly on the main road north from Antalya, a good journey breaker. They have an extensive series of interlinked caves with underwater lakes and stalactites. Also near Antalya, 30km (18¹/₂ miles) to

the northwest, are the **Karain Caves**. At Alanya under the promontory rock are the **Damlatafl Caves** with stalactites.

4x4 safaris

These exciting off-road experiences are great fun as routes lead down riverbeds, through farmland and into the Turkish hinterland. Most major resorts have a company which operates the safaris. Visit the local tourist office for details.

Waterparks

Waterparks have sprung up in most of the major resorts along the Aegean and Mediterranean coasts, and these make the perfect place to spend an afternoon.

At Kuşadası, you'll find **Adaland** at Çam Limani (5km/3 miles north of town), **Aqualand** on Long Beach and **Aquafantasy** at Pamuçak Beach.

Antalya plays host to **Aqualand Antalya** at Dunlupinar Bulvari, and there's also **Alanya Aquapark** at the Dedeman Hotel.

White-water rafting

Older children will love the ride down the Köprülü River, a two- to four-hour trip over exciting but not extreme rapids. For a more sedate experience you can kayak along the same route.

Zoos

Antalya has a little zoo in the clifftop **Karaalı Park**. Istanbul has a small zoo in the **Gülhane Park** situated below the Topkapı Palace.

Sport and leisure

For sports and outdoor enthusiasts a vast range of sport and leisure activities covering all seasons is available in Turkey. The best times of year to enjoy the great outdoors are generally April to May and September to October, when the heat of high summer is tempered. Whatever time of year, always carry ample water to avoid dehydration.

Ballooning

Flights over the lunar landscapes of Cappadocia, daily, early in the morning, with champagne on landing. *Kapadoyka Balloons, TR-50108 Nevşehir. Tel: (384) 271 2442; www.kapadokyaballoons.com*

Cycling

Organised cycle tours are available in Cappadocia and involve visits to some of the remoter churches and valleys, with fair amounts of walking required where terrain is not suitable for bicycles. Tours are also offered at Bodrum, Kuşadası, Marmaris and Turgutreis. **Argeus Tourism and Travel** (*Istiklal Caddesi 7, 50400 Ürgüp; tel: (384) 341 4688; www.argeus.com.tr*) offers a range of organised tours and holidays including cycle tours of Cappadocia.

Football (soccer)

Turkish teams are some of the strongest in Europe, but the best, Galatasaray and Fenerbahçe, are located in Istanbul and tickets are difficult to obtain.

Horse riding

Cappadocia is the most popular region for this, and riding is an excellent way to explore the valleys. Short tours of less than a day can be arranged locally, but for longer holidays involving camping out, it is best to book an organised tour (usually about ten people) from your own country. Horse riding is also available at Bodrum, Kuşadası, Ölü Deniz and Side.

Mountaineering

See also p146.
Specialist tour operators are:
Adventure Center
1311 63rd St, Emeryville CA 94608 USA Tel: (510) 654 1879; www.adventure-center.com
Exodus
9 Wier Rd, London SW12 0LT, UK. Tel: 020 8675 5550. www.exodus.co.uk

Explore Worldwide

1 Frederick St, Aldershot, Hampshire
GU11 1LQ, UK. Tel: 01252 760000;
www.explore.co.uk

Rafting

This can be practised in the Black Sea region on the Berhal, Berta, Çoruh, Fırtına, Hurşit and Oltu rivers, and in the Mediterranean region the Cehennem stream and the Dragon, Göksu, Köprüçay and Manavgat rivers.
Alternatifraft: Kenen Evren Bulvari,
Camlik Sokak 10/1, Marmaris. Tel: (252)
417 2920; www.alternatifraft.com

Scuba diving

At Bodrum, Fethiye and at Turunç Bay there are professional diving centres catering for beginners and advanced divers. A five-day course leads to an internationally recognised diving certificate.
Aegean Pro-dive: Neyzen Tevfk Caddesi
212, Bodrum. Tel: (252) 316 0737;
www.aegeanprodive.com

Skiing

Uludağ, 34km (21 miles) from Bursa, is Turkey's premier ski resort at 1,900m (6,200ft), with slopes for beginners and intermediates. There are 25–30 pisted runs and lots of off-piste, six chairlifts and six T-bar lifts. Lifts are open 9am– dusk and the season is from December to the end of April.
Pistes are deserted midweek, but get busier at weekends. The standard of hotels is high.

Skiing at small resorts is also available.
Simply Turkey: King's House, Wood St,
Kingston-upon-Thames.
Tel: (0208) 541 2204;
www.simplytravel.com

Tennis

Tennis courts are available in the resorts of Antalya, Bodrum, Fethiye, Gümbet, İçmeler, Kemer, Kuşadası, Ölü Deniz, Marmaris and Side.

Water sports

All Turkish coastal resorts have an excellent range of water sports including banana riding, paragliding, parascending, surfboarding, waterskiing, windsurfing and jetskiing. For specific information about what's available at any given resort contact the local tourist office, but in general Alanya, Altınkum, Bodrum, Fethiye, Gümbet, İçmeler, Kemer, Kuşadası, Marmaris, Side and Turunç will have the full range. The main beach at Ölü Deniz has powered water sports but these aren't allowed in the lagoon. You can only kayak, pedalo, snorkel and swim here.

Yachting

There are fully equipped yachting marinas from north to south at Istanbul, Çanakkale, Çeşme, Siğacık, Kuşadası, Bodrum, Datça, Marmaris, Göçek, Fethiye, Kalkan, Kaş, Finike, Kemer and Antalya. Foreign flagged yachts are allowed to sail in or between Turkish ports free of charge provided the yacht owner is on board.

Food and drink

Turkish cuisine ranks with French and Chinese as one of the great cuisines of the world. Eating out is a national pastime that Turks take seriously and derive great pleasure from at the same time. As a result, there is an endless variety of eating places on offer, all very good value, and since Turkey grows all its own produce the quality and freshness are excellent.

Types of eating and drinking places

Gazino: as above plus entertainment.

Içkili lokanta: as above but licensed for alcohol.

Kahve: a coffee house, usually men only, serving coffee and tea.

Kebapçi: serving various Turkish grilled meats.

Lokanta: an informal restaurant serving home-cooked Turkish meals with non-alcoholic drinks.

Pideci: Turkish pizza parlour.

Restoran: a more formal restaurant serving international as well as Turkish dishes, with alcohol.

In eating places where food is displayed, choose from the display rather than the menu. In *lokantas* there is often no menu, and you need to go to the kitchen to choose.

In restaurants a 10 or 15 per cent service charge is normally added to your bill, but it is usual to leave an extra 5 per cent for the waiter. In *lokantas* no service is added, so leave 10 per cent. Istanbul, as ever, offers the biggest range and best-quality eating places in the country, with some extremely sophisticated restaurants, many with Bosporus views. Prices for a meal without alcohol range from cheap in the simple *lokantas* to expensive in the top places. As you travel eastwards, the food and eating places become less good and less varied, but prices drop accordingly.

What to eat
Turkish cuisine

The most exciting thing in Turkish food is the *meze*, the delicious range of little appetisers which can either be a meal in themselves or the forerunner to the main course. It is in these *meze* that Turkish cooks use their imagination and creativity to dream up, for instance, 101 things to do with an aubergine. They are excellent for vegetarians as they consist of such items as *börek* (small pastry cases filled with cheese and herbs), *dolma* (vine leaves stuffed with rice), aubergine dips and salads, yoghurt and garlic dips.

Olive oil is a key ingredient in all Turkish food, and some may find the food rather oily. Others swear by it and are convinced it is the secret of the lush hair growth enjoyed in all Mediterranean countries. Great care is taken with presentation and each little dish will be garnished with parsley, lemon or olives. Freshly baked Turkish bread (*pide*) is supplied with *meze* in limitless amounts.

With four seas washing the shorelines, fish is another key ingredient, with treated fish titbits like *hamsi* (anchovies) forming part of a *meze*, while for main courses there is sea bass, bonito, swordfish, squid, giant prawns, red bream, striped bream, gurnard and striped goatfish. Fish is generally more expensive than meat, unless you seek out some of the *lokantas* in Kumkapı. Riverfish, as at Bafa, Eğridir, Iznik and Manavgat, is particularly good value and is always fresh.

Baking bread in Cappadocia

Lamb is the most popular meat, used in the well-known *şiş kebab* and *döner kebab*, but also made into spiced meatballs (*köfte*). Chicken is used less often, but is very tasty when prepared with walnuts, garlic and paprika as in Circassian chicken.

Accompaniments to main courses are usually rice (*pilav*) – often served with pine nuts, currants, spices and salads.

Desserts, apart from fresh fruit and ice cream, tend to be extremely sweet, as in delicate milk puddings scented with rosewater or honey-soaked pastries garnished with nuts, and have names like Lady's Navel, Nightingale's Nest and Minister's Finger.

A sample Turkish menu in a good restaurant might read as follows:

Mezeler (hors d'oeuvres)
Arnavut ciğeri: spicy fried liver with onions
Çerkes tavuğu: cold chicken in walnut purée with garlic
Çiğ köfte: spicy meatballs
Midye dolması: stuffed mussels
Yaprak dolması: stuffed vine leaves

Çorbalar (soups)
Yala çorbası: yogurt soup
Düğün çorbası: meat soup with egg yolks stirred in
Ikembe çorbası: tripe soup

Izgaralar (grilled meats)
Bonfile: fillet steak
Döner kebab: lamb grilled on a revolving spit

Pirzola: lamb chops
Şiş kebab: grilled lamb on skewers
Iskender kebab: lamb pieces in tomato and yoghurt sauce
Şiş köfte: grilled meatballs

Pilavlar (rices)
Sade pilav: plain rice pilaf
Iç pilav: rice with pine nuts, currants and onions
Bulgur pilavı: cracked wheat pilaf

**Zeytinyağlılar
(cold vegetables in olive oil)**
Imam bayıldı: split aubergine with tomatoes and onions
Kabak kızartması: fried baby marrow slices with yoghurt
Patlıcan kızartması: fried aubergine slices with yoghurt
Zeytinyağlı fasulye: green beans in tomato sauce

Börekler (savoury pastries)
Sigara börek: fried filo pastry filled with cheese
Talaş böreği: puff pastry filled with meat

Salatalar (salads)
Cacık: chopped cucumber in yoghurt with garlic
Çoban salata: mixed tomato, pepper, cucumber and onion
Patlıcan salatası: puréed aubergine salad
Piyaz: haricot bean salad

Tatlılar (desserts)
Baklava: flaky pastry stuffed with nuts in honey syrup

Pavement cafés serve alcohol

Tel kadayıf: shredded wheat stuffed with nuts in syrup
Sütlaç: creamy cold rice pudding
Komposto: cold stewed fruit
Dondurma: ice cream
Meyvalar: fruits

The standard Turkish breakfast consists of freshly baked bread, white goat's cheese, black olives, tomatoes, yoghurt, honey and jam, with sweet black tea.

For snacks, there are kiosks in all cities selling things like *lahmacun*, thin pizza with minced meat on top, rolled up and eaten like an ice cream cone, or *köfte* and salad stuffed into pitta bread.

Other simple village items are *gözleme* (Turkish stuffed pancake) and *manti*

A LITTLE AT A TIME

Because most Turks enjoy a meal of several dishes at once – a *meze* – many traditional *lokantas* or restaurants will bring whatever you order to the table at the same time. If you want to enjoy several courses in the western style it's best to order one course at a time.

(Turkish ravioli). Turkey now caters for the fast-food and chips fans as well.

International cuisine

Although Turkish cuisine remains dominant throughout the country, Istanbul and the tourist resorts along the coast offer a fair range of international cuisine, often served in restaurants opened by expats from Britain, Germany or France.

You are sure to be able to find good options at the 5-star branded hotels such as the Sheraton and Hilton, though prices will be accordingly high. At the other end of the scale national predilections such as the English breakfast can be catered for at resorts such as Kuşadası or Ölü-Deniz.

What to drink

Alcoholic

Most people are surprised to discover that Turkey is the world's sixth-largest wine producer. The word 'wine' even originated from the Hittite language.

Turkish wine (both red and white) is good. The best reds are Yakut, Buzbağ and Villa Doluca, and the best white is Çankaya. There is also the *rosé* Lâl, and the *primeur* Nevşehir. Also recommended is the Special Reserve Karmen and the semi-sweet Vadı.

Beer is the locally produced Efes, good and reasonably priced.

Rakı, an aniseed spirit, is the national alcoholic drink, usually mixed with ice and water, when it goes cloudy. *Rakı* goes well with *meze* and with fish, and

Turks generally drink it as an accompaniment to food rather than by itself as an aperitif.

Non-alcoholic

Ayran is the national non-alcoholic drink, a chilled, unsweetened thin yoghurt, an acquired taste, but very thirst-quenching and refreshing.

Mineral waters are cheap and excellent and come both fizzy and still. Even locals drink them in preference to the tap water as they taste so much better.

The usual range of fizzy drinks such as Coca-Cola or fizzy lemonade (Sprite or Yedigün) is available. Street stalls also sell freshly squeezed juices like orange, carrot and apple.

Tea and coffee

Turkish coffee (*kahve*) is drunk to finish a meal or at any time of day, served in tiny cups. While ordering you should specify the sugar level: *sade* (no sugar), *az* (little sugar), *orta* (medium sugar), *çok şekerli* (lots of sugar).

Tea (*çay*) is drunk at any time, served black in little glasses on saucers, with a tiny spoon for stirring in the sugar lumps.

HOT OR COLD

Turks don't enjoy their food piping hot, and most servings will come warm – not the best way to enjoy items like French fries! Although they may have a little smile at your desire for hot food, most restaurants will be happy to accommodate your request.

Food and drink

Where to eat

★   under 10 YTL
★★   from 11–20 YTL
★★★   from 21–40 YTL
★★★★   over 40 YTL

In the restaurant listings below, the following symbols have been used to indicate the average cost of a meal per person, not including alcohol.

Many Turkish hotels also have restaurants (some insist on charging half board, certainly in high season); however, with a few exceptions in eastern Turkey, it is better to eat at a restaurant. Certainly the food will be cheaper and the atmosphere more authentic.

In eastern Turkey the reverse is true and there will probably be little choice other than your hotel restaurant in which to enjoy a full meal.

Turkish cuisine provides so much food that is naturally vegetarian with its excellent range of *meze* starters that there is not a market for specific vegetarian restaurants. Based on tomatoes, aubergines, salads, chick peas, spinach and cheese pastries, the selection is enough to satisfy even the pickiest vegetarian.

ISTANBUL

Amedros ★★
European-style bistro that also offers some interesting Ottoman dishes.
Hoca Rustem Sokak 7, off Divan Yolu, Sultanahmet.
Tel: (212) 522 8356.

Sesame bread rings for sale

Cennet ★
A traditional tea and snack house where the staff wear Ottoman costumes and there's live music throughout the day. Although it's a little overdone, Turks come here as well as tourists because the food is good.
Divanyölü Caddesi.

Changa ★★★
Fine dining in the business district, this is one of the trendiest for fusion food.
Siraselviler Caddesi 87/1, Taksim.
Tel: (212) 249 1348.

Çiçek Pasaji ★★
This former flower market in Galatasaray district is renowned for its collection of good-value typical restaurants, though some feel it has become a victim of its own success because it has become so popular with tourists.
Istiklal Caddesi, Beyoğlu.

Darüzziyafe ★★

Respected and long-standing Turkish restaurant serving Ottoman cuisine in lovely open courtyard setting amongst the buildings of the Sulimaniye Mosque.

Darüşşifa Sokak, Beyazit.

Kumkapı ★/★★

Not one restaurant but a waterside district where fresh fish is hauled ashore direct to hundreds of small stalls and restaurants, some with live music and belly dancing. The food is excellent and cheap. A great atmosphere.

On the waterfront 2km (1¼ miles) west of Sultanahmet.

Leb-i-Derya ★★★

International cuisine and breathtaking views over the Bosporus. Open terrace in summer, open fire in winter.

Kumbaraci Yokusu 115/7 Tunel, Beyoglu.

Tel: (212) 293 4989.

Pandeli ★★★

Renowned restaurant set in the Spice or Egyptian market with excellent food and with seating in tiled alcoves.

Mısır Çarşışı, Eminönü.

Open: lunch only.

Closed: Sun.

Rami ★★★

Classy place offering traditional cuisine and panoramic views from an old Ottoman house.

Utangac Sokak 6, Cankurtaran.

Tel: (212) 517 6593.

Şark Khavasi ★

Take a rest during your tour of the Grand Bazaar at this authentic Turkish coffee shop. You'll also be able to try a *hookah* (tobacco pipe in which smoke is drawn through water, also known as a 'hubble bubble' pipe).

Yağıkcılar Caddesi, Kapalıçarflı.

Seasons Restaurant ★★★★

One of Istanbul's finest and classiest options for international cuisine, set in an elegant glass pavilion.

Four Seasons Hotel, Tevkikhane Sokak 1.

Tel: (212) 638 8200.

Sultanahmet Köftecisi ★

A cafeteria-style eatery with a good standard of Turkish food. Good budget option for central Sultanahmet, well known for excellent *köfte* (meatballs).

Divanyölü Caddesi 28.

AEGEAN REGION

Afrodisias

Aphrodisias Hotel ★★

It's the only place to eat close to the ancient excavated site, but this French/Turkish-owned hotel serves food with that little extra touch of Gallic '*je ne sais quoi*'.

Opposite the site entrance, Afrodisias.

Ayvalık

Diniz Restaurant ★★

Famed *meyhane* (traditional inn) with excellent salads and *meze* in addition to grilled fish.

At the port.

Milky glasses of raki

Bafa Gölü
Zeybeks ★
This tiny restaurant/café is open throughout the day and offers simple food and wine in the evenings. The owner will also serenade you with his guitar.
Bafa Gölü.

Bodrum
Denizhan ★★
Best place to enjoy typical Turkish cuisine and Turkish balloon bread (*lavash*), then excellent *meze*, on the outskirts of town.
Denizhan, Et Lokantasi, Konacik.
Tel: (252) 363 7674.

Secret Garden ★★★
Tasty Mediterranean food prepared by English owner/chef. Comfortable chairs in a romantic garden down a small side street opposite the marina.
Eskicesme Mah. Danaci Sokak 20.
Tel: (252) 313 1641.

Datça
Hüsnünün Yeri ★★
Located directly on the waterfront of this tiny bay and much loved by

Enjoy a meal alfresco

'yachties'. It offers some of the freshest seafood around. This is an excellent place to while away an afternoon.
Waterfront Datça.

Our Place ★★
Good choice for vegetarian and natural food – though there are some meat dishes for die-hard meat eaters.
Hisarönü.

Kuşadası
Carvansarai Restaurant ★★★
The atmospheric courtyard setting of this fine restaurant is matched by the food, which includes European

dishes. There are regular folkloric evenings.
Carvansarai Hotel, Atatürk Bulvari.

Kutes Kafeteria ★★
Overlooking the cruise port and the bottom of the old town, this is the place to join locals having a drink.
Town waterfront, Atatürk Bulvari.

Pamukkale
Weisse Burg ★★
A popular spot for foreigners and tourists to hang out (there are also cheap rooms). The food is tasty and good value.
Menderes Caddesi.

MEDITERRANEAN REGION

Aspendos
Belkis ★★
Set beside a Byzantine bridge just south of Aspendos, Belkis makes a reliable lunch stop on your tours. There's a terrace on the water's edge.
On the road to Aspendos from the N400 coast road.

Dalyan
Lei Lei ★/★★
Five kilometres (3 miles) from town on the main road, this large restaurant serves a good range of Turkish meat and seafood. It also has nesting storks in the early summer and a range of ducks and pond life which fascinate children.
On the main road out of town towards Ortaca.

Fethiye
Les Jardins de Levissi ★★
A French/Turkish couple bought this mansion in the deserted village of Kayaköy and they provide delicious food and a splendidly relaxing place to stay.
Küyübaflı mevkii Kayaköyu.

Kaş
Chez Evi ★★★
In the 1980s Evi, a Frenchwoman, chose Kafl as her new home, and this restaurant set up by her serves excellent French cuisine and is now an institution in the resort.
Terzi Sokak.

ANATOLIA

Ankara
Budakalti ★★★
An old four-storey house located in the southern suburb of Gaziosmanpasha, Budakalti offers a synthesis of Italian and Turkish cuisine such as warm almond and chicken salad.
Budakalti Caddesi.
Tel: (312) 219 1020.

Cicek Lokantesi ★★
Long-standing restaurant with family-style cooking, situated in the old citadel. It is very popular with a faithful Turkish clientele.
Çankyry C 12/A, Uluş.

Goksu ★★★★
With a menu of excellent Black Sea cuisine (concentrating on fish transported from that sea-coast region daily), this is one of Ankara's most renowned restaurants.
Bayındır Sokak 22A, Kızılay.
Tel: (312) 431 2219.
Reservations essential.

Marco Polo ★★★★
Fine international dining as befits the reputation of this 5-star hotel. The menu is ever-changing and features a good-value daily special and themed Turkish evenings.
Hilton Hotel, Tahran Caddesi 12, Kavaklıdere, Ankara.
Tel: (312) 467 3154.
Reservations required.

Cappadocia
Bizin Ev ★★
Two beautifully restored stone mansions now offer four different dining rooms with a range of traditional low seating to formal dining. Lovely atmosphere. The place is open all year round.
Orta Mah, Baclacı Sokak 1, Avanos.

Hotels and accommodation

The standard of accommodation in Turkey covers the full range from five-star de luxe Hiltons and Sheratons in the cities right through to simple family-run pensions in the towns and villages. At all levels standards are improving year by year.

This is definitely not the Middle East with its malfunctioning equipment and power cuts, but neither is it Europe with its immaculate plumbing and efficient chambermaids. Turkey falls somewhere in between. Service is invariably friendly and willing, and many of the newer hotels are imaginatively designed, following traditional styles.

Along the Aegean and western Mediterranean coasts, the demand from international tourism has meant a constant expansion in accommodation over the last 30 years. Though there are still many dour concrete box-type hotels there is also the option of a new range of 'boutique' style hotels, often housed in renovated Ottoman houses or built in traditional style.

As a general rule, the further east you travel the less sophisticated the accommodation, but there are many simple family pensions throughout the country offering acceptable, spotlessly clean rooms.

Grading of hotels

The grading of hotels is carried out by the Ministry of Culture and Tourism. However, the system is confusing and cannot be compared 'like for like' with grading systems in other countries and many good hotels choose not to be registered.

Five-star equivalent: a luxury hotel with full facilities.
Four-star equivalent: a very good hotel with above-average facilities.
Three-star equivalent: a good tourist hotel with a moderate level of comfort.
Two-star equivalent: a simpler hotel with a moderate level of comfort, which may not have a dining room.
One-star equivalent: a modest hotel or pension with simple facilities, usually offering just bed and breakfast and often with shared bathroom and toilet. Five- and four-star hotels always have a TV and mini-bar in the rooms, as do many three-star hotels. Two-star and below do not. Price fluctuations in

the two- and three-star categories are considerable, often for no discernible reason.

Useful information

Many large hotels make half-board compulsory, so establish the basis of the pricing system before comparing hotels.

Because of fluctuations in the value of the Turkish lira, hotels price rooms in various other currencies. Dollars and euros are the most common, though some price in pounds sterling.

Rates in the better hotels are high, so it pays to pre-book or even explore travel packages, especially if you only intend to travel within a defined region of Turkey.

Hot water is generally provided by solar heating and may be in short supply in the mornings, early and late

Turkey has accommodation to offer for everyone

in the season. Water should always be used sparingly, whatever the season. Most Turkish hotels won't have bath or sink plugs – this is because of the Muslim custom of cleansing under running water. Remember to pack your own!

Accommodation in eastern Turkey is far more limited than the rest of the country. Each large town tends to have two or three two- or three-star hotels, and, if they happen to be full, the gap in standard to the next hotel/pension can be enormous. It is best to be flexible in outlook or book ahead, particularly in summer.

Camping

There is a wide range of campsites in Turkey, even though simple pensions are so very cheap. Campsites cost very little per night and often have permanent tents erected with beds or simple chalet accommodation. Rough camping is a wonderful way to appreciate the beauty of some of the mountain areas where no other accommodation exists.

Where to stay

The following list of suggested hotels will help you select an appropriate place to suit your budget.

Note: YTL = Yeni Türk Lirası (New Turkish Lira)

★   Budget under 95 YTL

★★   Moderate/standard 96–185 YTL

★★★   Expensive over 185 YTL

ISTANBUL
Çirağan Palace
Hotel ★★★
Expensive yet exquisite Çirağan is a renovated palace on the waterfront with a top-class range of amenities including excellent restaurants and bars.
Çirağan Caddesi 32, Beşiktaş.
Tel: (212) 258 3377;
www.ciraganpalace.com
Celal Sultan Hotel ★★
Elegant, stylish hotel with roof garden and restaurant within easy walking distance of Aya Sofya, the Topkapı, etc.
Yerebatan Caddesi

Salkimsogut Sokak 16, 34410 Sultanahmet.
Tel: (212) 520 9323/4;
www.celalsultan.com
Garden House Hotel ★★
Former fisherman's house, cosy ambience, friendly, helpful staff, restaurant and wireless internet.
Kucuk Ayasofya Mahalesi, Sehit Mehmet Pasha Sokak 11/13, 34400 Sultanahmet.
Tel: (212) 517 9111; www. gardenhouseistanbul.com
Pera Palas ★★★
The faded grandeur of the Orient Express gives this place its special ambience.

Mesrutiyet Caddesi 98/100, Tepebasi.
Tel: (212) 2514560;
www.perapalas.com
Turkuaz Hotel ★★
This beautifully restored 19th-century Ottoman house has 12 rooms and a restaurant.
Kadirga Cinci Meydani 36, 34400 Sultanahmet.
Tel: (212) 5160862;
www.hotelturkuaz.com

AEGEAN COAST
Afrodisias
Aphrodisias Hotel ★★
This small hotel cum restaurant is owned by French/Turkish proprietors who bring a

The well-planned and beautifully designed resort town of Kemer

Many of the pensions in Kalkan have roof terraces

touch of chic to the simple décor. Excellent budget option.
Karacasu Caddesi, Afrodisias.
Tel: (0256) 448 8132; fax: (0256) 448 8422.

Bafa Gölü (Lake Bafa)
Club Natura Oliva ★★
Bungalows set in an olive grove on the banks of Lake Bafa – this is an eco-friendly resort. Local produce is served for breakfast and the hotel will organise walking tours of the area.
Kocaorman Mah. Pinarcik Koyu, Lake Bafa.
Tel: (0252) 519 1072; fax: (0252) 519 1015.
Open: May–Oct.

Bodrum
Hotel Belvedere ★★
Attractive design with castellations, 130 rooms, large pool, restaurant. 50km (31 miles) from the airport.
Cumhuriyet Caddesi Erdemir Sokak 5, Yalikavak.
Tel: (252) 3852214; www.vivahotels.com.tr
Blue Dolphin Hotel ★
Simple 26-room place on the beach, 2 restaurants, 30km (18¹/₂ miles) from the airport.
Ataturk Caddesi 120, Torba.
Tel: (252) 3671049; email: bodrumbluedolphin@ hotmail.com

Bozcaada (Dardenelles)
Kaikas Hotel ★★
This new neoclassical-style hotel is popular with the fashionable Turks who weekend in the area. Thus it has extra touches such as a good wine bar.
Kale Arkası, Bozcaada, Çanakkale.
Tel: (0286) 697 0250; fax: (0286) 697 8857.

Foça
Stone House ★★
Renovated stone mansion with three rooms and kitchen for B&B. You can rent the whole complex for a week or two.

*Sokak 11, Foça. Tel:
(0232) 812 1244; winter
tel: (+43 1) 712 1951.
Open: Apr–Oct.*

Izmir

Antik Han Hotel ★★

Beautifully renovated
old inn in the heart
of Izmir.
*Anarfartlar C 600
Mezarlikbasi, Izmir.
Tel: (0232) 489 2750;
fax: (0232) 483 5925.*

MEDITERRANEAN COAST

Adrasan (Olymbos)

Eviniz Pansiyon ★

German/Turkish family-
owned guesthouse, set
up in a traditional
country house but with
a good pool and terrace.

This is the quietest
corner of the western
Turkish coast.
*Deniz C 540, Çavuşköy,
Kumlaça.
Tel: (242) 883 1110.*

Antakya

Savon ★

This former soap factory
makes an unusual shell for
a small but unique hotel,
furnished with an eclectic
modern décor, surprising
for this part of Turkey.
*Kurtulus Caddesi 192.
Tel: (326) 214 6355.*

Antalya

Tuvana Hotel ★★★

Situated in the old town,
this characterful hotel
combines luxury with a
cosy atmosphere. There

is a beautiful courtyard
and large pool.
*Tuzcular M Karanlık
S 18, Kaleiçi.
Tel: (242) 244 4054;
www.tuvanahotel.com*

Dalyan

Happy Caretta Hotel ★

With an excellent view of
the Lycian tombs from its
riverside location, the
Happy Caretta is a family-
owned budget base, set
in a shady garden.
*Maraş Caddesi Ada.
Tel: (252) 284 2109.*

Fethiye

Les Jardins de Levissi ★★

A French/Turkish couple
bought this mansion in
the deserted village of
Kayaköy for a splendid

An attractive hotel terrace in Cappadocia

relaxing place to tour the region. They also provide delicious food.
Küyübaşi mevkii Kayköyü.
Tel: (252) 618 0188.

Kalkan
Club Xanthos ★★★
Exclusive 70-room hotel with two restaurants, large pool, sauna and disco.
Kalamar Koyu, 07960 Kalkan.
Tel: (242) 844 2388;
www.clubxanthos.com

Kalkan Han ★
Small but smart *pansiyon* – one of the very first that was established in this coastal resort which took aesthetics into account when planning rooms. These are simple yet stylish, though not all rooms have A/C.
Kalkan Köy.
Tel: (0242) 844 3151;
fax: (242) 844 2059.
Open: May–Oct.

Kaş
Club Capa Hotel ★★★
Rising majestically out of the verdant forest just above the water, Club Capa offers its own lido in addition to a pool.

It is out of town so better for visitors with their own transport.
Cukurbağ Yaramadası.
Tel: (242) 836 3190.

ANKARA AND EASTERN TURKEY
Ankara
Gordion Hotel ★★/★★★
A small luxury hotel, with European-style décor and an English-style bar. Indoor pool, sauna.
Tunalı Hilmi Caddesi, Büklüm S 59.
Tel: (312) 427 8080;
www.gordionhotel.com

Cappadocia
Museum Hotel ★★★
With a combination of modern packaged in traditional style and cave rooms, the Museum offers interesting, eclectically furnished luxury accommodation.
Tekelli Mah 1,Üçhisar.
Tel: (0384) 219 2220;
fax: (0384) 219 2444.
Open: year round.

BLACK SEA COAST
Barhal/Artvin
Karahan Pensiyon ★
At the southern base for Mount Kaçkar, this

remote pension sits in wild countryside. Clean, simple accommodation.
Altıparmak Köyü, Yüsüfeli.
Tel: (466) 826 2071.

Gaziantep
Antik Belkis Hotel ★★
A wonderfully characterful stone house, refurbished by a painter and political activist.
Kayacık Ara S16, Şahinbey.
Tel: (342) 231 1084.

Mardin
Erdoba Houses ★
In the maze of streets in the old town are two mansions, now comprising a lovely small hotel and a private home for a family or group to rent.
Bırıncı Caddesi 135.
Tel: (482) 212 7787.

Nemrut Dağı
Euphrat Hotel ★
In the shadow of Nemrut Dağ, this basic hotel offers budget accommodation but exquisite views.
Karadut Köyü Kahta, Adyaman.
Tel: (416) 737 2175.

On business

Business centres

Most large international hotels in the main cities will offer services to business clients, including internet access, faxing, copying, rooms for meetings, etc. There is a fully equipped business centre at the British Chamber of Commerce and the Ankara Business Centre at the Ankara Hilton, which has an international staff (*Tahran Caddesi 12, 06700 Kavaklıdere; tel: (0312) 428 6177; fax: (0312) 428 6179; www.abcentre.com*).

Bank accounts

Foreigners may keep their foreign currency in a Foreign Exchange Deposit Account in any bank authorised to exchange foreign currency.

Bribery

Anyone found offering any sort of bribe, money or gifts, especially to a government employee, is liable to imprisonment.

Business hours

Banks
Mon–Fri 8.30am–noon & 1.30–6pm.
Business offices
Mon–Fri 8.30am–5.30pm or 9am–6pm.
Government offices
Mon–Fri 8.30am–12.30pm & 1.30–5.30pm.

Business visas

Business visitors are given 90-day visas, issued at the point of entry.

Capital investment

Foreigners may invest foreign capital in Turkey as hard currency, tangible fixed assets (eg, machinery, tools) or intangible fixed assets (eg, patents, trademarks). Income generated from any business, in the form of sales revenues or dividends, for example, may be reinvested. The minimum investment is currently £50,000.

Any transactions related to the use of foreign capital come under the discretion of the State Planning Organisation's Foreign Capital Department. All foreigners wanting to initiate business operations in Turkey must obtain permission from this body.

Chambers of commerce

Ankara Chamber of Commerce
Şehit Teğmen Kalmaz Caddesi 30, Ankara. Tel: 310 4145; fax: 310 8436; www.ato.org.tr
The British Chamber of Commerce in Turkey
Mesrutiyat Caddesi 18, Asly Han Kat 6, Galatasaray. Tel: 249 0658; fax: 242 5551; www.bcct.org.tr
Istanbul Chamber of Commerce
Istanbul Chamber Resadiye Caddesi, 34112 Eminönü. Tel: (0212) 455 6000; fax: (0212) 513 1565; www.tr-ito.org
Izmir Chamber of Commerce
Izmir Chamber PO box 77, Izmir 3520. Tel: (232) 441 7777; fax: (232) 441 6528; www.izto.org.tr

There are also Chambers of Commerce at Adana, Balıkesir, Bursa, Denizli, Eskişehir, Gaziantep, Iskenderun, Izmit, Kayseri, Mersin and Samsun.

Conference facilities

Many four- and five-star hotels aim to attract conference business because of the high revenue it generates, and there is a great deal of competition between hotels, particularly in Istanbul. Packages can be tailored to specific needs. Consult the hotel marketing department.

Etiquette

Business cards are a must at introductions. It is very important in Turkey to establish a good personal relationship first, allowing time for friendly chat before embarking on business topics.

Government contracts

Most government business is centred on Ankara and is conducted on the public tender system. It is essential to have competent local representation.

Language

Most business people and levels of upper management will speak some English and possibly German; however, it is certainly appreciated if you speak at least a few phrases of Turkish. Trade literature may be in English, French or German, but technical catalogues or leaflets must be printed in Turkish.

Market research

A long-established market research company is TNS Piar in Istanbul *Tel: (212) 337 3400; fax: (216) 336 9067; www.tns-global.com.tr*

Premises

Real estate agents are listed in the newspapers. For Sale *(satılık)* or For Rent *(kıralık)* notices are put up on vacant buildings and apartments.

Residence and work permits

Called a *kimlik*, a residence permit is required by foreigners wanting to stay longer than three months. The maximum duration is two years.

Work permits are required by foreigners. Permission is obtained from the security authorities.

Tax

All legitimately working foreigners are exempt from income tax. Those whose residence is in Turkey or who live in Turkey for more than six consecutive months must pay tax.

Useful addresses

EU Commission: *Uğar Mumcu Caddesi 88, Kat 4, Gaziomanpaşa, Ankara. Tel: (312) 446 5511; fax: (312) 446 6737.*
Turkish British Cultural Institute: *Bestekar Sokak 32, Kavaklıdere, Ankara. Tel: (312) 419 1844; fax: (312) 418 5404 & Istiklal Caddesi, Ö.R.S. Turiskik Iş Hanı 251–253, Beyoğlu, Istanbul. Tel: (212) 252 7474; fax: (212) 252 8682.*
Turkish American Association: *Cinnah Caddesi 20, Çankaya, Ankara. Tel: (312) 426 2648; fax: (312) 468 2538.*

Practical guide

Arriving

Visas are required by British and Irish nationals and South Africans. They can be bought on entry and are valid for three months. They cost £10, payable in foreign currency, with no change given. Visas are not required for visitors holding Australian, Canadian, New Zealand or American passports.

By air
Istanbul

Atatürk Istanbul Airport, where most international flights arrive, is the country's busiest, located at Yeşilköy, 25km (15½ miles) west of the city centre. A taxi to the centre takes 30 minutes and is reasonably priced. There are cheaper Turkish Airlines buses every hour to Şişhane in the centre, but they do not stop en route. Onward flights to North Cyprus (Ercan) depart from the international terminal, while the transit flights to other cities situated within Turkey depart from the normal domestic terminal. easyJet has flights from Luton and Basel to Istanbul.

Other cities

Ankara and Izmir are the other two main airports receiving scheduled international flights. Izmir airport (Adnan Menderes) is 30km (18½ miles) south of the city, and Ankara (Esenboğa) is 28km (17½ miles) north of the centre.

Bodrum/Milas, Dalaman and Antalya, take charter flights.

By bus

There are regular bus services to Istanbul from all European capitals, and the direct route via the western Balkans is now safe again, so there is no need to go the long way round via Romania or Hungary.

By car

No special documents are required for visits of under three months. The car is entered on the driver's passport as imported goods and must be driven out again in time. For stays of over three months, contact the **Turkish Touring Club (TTOK)**, Saniayi Sitesi Yanı 4 (*tel: (0212) 282 8140; www.touring.org.tr*) to obtain a Carnet de Passage.

By rail

There are daily departures to Istanbul from all European capitals. From London the journey takes three nights. The two commonest routes are via Paris, Vienna, Budapest and Bucharest or via Paris, Vienna, Belgrade and Sofia. Another option is via Athens and Thessaloniki, or via Italy then catching a ferry from Ancona or Brindisi. For up-to-date details of rail services, consult the *Thomas Cook European Timetable* (published monthly, available from UK branches of Thomas Cook or *tel: 01733 416477*).

Watching cruise ships from a roadside café affords a welcome break

By sea

There are three ways to arrive in Turkey by boat. First from Venice, Italy. **Turkish Maritime Lines (TML)** (*tel: (0212) 245 5366*) operate comfortable car ferries from April to October, running once a week to Izmir. Second, from North Cyprus (*see p142*). Third, from the Greek islands (*see pp142–3*). For details, see *www.tour-turkey.com/greece-and-turkey-ferries.htm*

Camping

There are numerous sites along the Aegean and Mediterranean coasts, a choice in Cappadocia, plus an excellent site close to the airport in Istanbul with good transport links into the city centre.

Campsites in Turkey always have a communal kitchen (sometimes an outside cooking area) in addition to electricity, toilets and wash-blocks with hot showers. These are of mixed cleanliness and modernity. All sites get crowded in peak season (July–Aug) when services can be stretched.

There are no campsites along the Black Sea coast or in the east of Turkey.

Children

Children are welcome almost everywhere – in hotels, restaurants and shops. Turkish Airlines (THY) offer the standard IATA child reductions; 90 per cent for under-twos and 50 per cent for two to twelves.

Climate

The best time to visit is between May and October. The tourist season in the coastal regions runs from 1 April to 31 October. July and August can be too hot for exploring sites in the midday sun.

Crime

Violent crime rates are low, as are petty crime rates, but it is always wise to take sensible precautions. In the event of a crime, report it to the Tourist Police (*see also p185*).

Customs regulations

On entry, duty-free limits are 200 cigarettes and 50 cigars, 200g (7oz) of tobacco, five 100cl (1^3/$_4$pt) or seven 70cl (1^1/$_4$pt) bottles of wine and/or spirits, five bottles of perfume, 120ml (4fl oz) maximum each. The import of all narcotics is forbidden and carries stiff

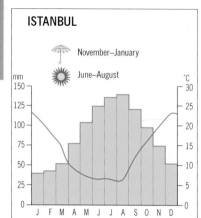

ISTANBUL

November–January

June–August

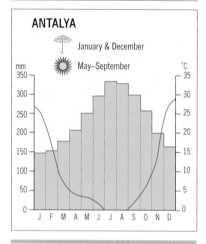

ANTALYA

January & December

May–September

**WEATHER CONVERSION
CHART**

25.4mm = 1 inch

°F = 1.8 × °C + 32

prison sentences. The export of
antiquities is forbidden. Proof of
purchase is required for a new
carpet, and a certificate detailing
age from a museum directorate for an
old carpet.

Driving

Car hire

This is expensive. Drivers must be over
21 and have a valid driving licence from
their own country. For insurance
details, see below.

Emergency

In the event of a breakdown, call the
Turkish Touring and Automobile Club
(Istanbul head office *tel: 282 8140;
fax: 282 8042*). If you are involved in an
accident, remember you must notify
the police.

Insurance

You should take out personal travel
insurance before departure, from a
travel agent, tour operator or insurance
company in your home country. It
should give adequate cover for medical
expenses, loss and theft, personal
liability (but liability arising from
motor accidents is not usually
included) and cancellation expenses.
You should personally check details of
exclusions, details of cover, and that the
amount of cover is adequate.

Motorists driving their own cars
should notify their home insurer to
extend third-party liability cover
to Turkey.

If you hire a car the collision
damage waiver (CDW) is normally
offered by the hirer, and is usually
compulsory. Check this detail with
your own motor insurers, as you may
already be covered by your policy.
If not, CDW is payable locally and may

be as much as 50 per cent of the hiring fee. Neither CDW nor your personal travel insurance, however, will protect you for liability arising from an accident in a hire car, for example, if you damage another vehicle or injure someone. If you are likely to hire a car, you should obtain such extra cover, preferably from your travel agent or other insurer before departure.

Petrol

The available types are super (four-star), normal (two-star), unleaded (only in cities and tourist areas) and diesel. There are plenty of petrol stations.

Roads

Turkey has a well-maintained road network. Traffic drives on the right and the Turkish highway code is very similar to the European.

Speed limits

In towns the speed limit is 50kph (31mph), on state highways it is 90kph (56mph) and on motorways 120kph (74mph).

Electricity

220 volts, 50 cycles and two-pin European plugs.

Embassies and consulates

Australia Ankara: Gaziosmanpafla, Nenehatun Caddesi No 83.
Tel: (312) 459 9500.
Istanbul: Etiler, Tepecik Yolu Uzeri No 58. *Tel: (212) 257 7050.*

Canada Ankara: Gaziosmanpafla, Nenehatun Caddesi No 75.
Tel: (312) 459 9200.
Istanbul: Istiklal Caddesi 373, Beyoğlu.
Tel: (212) 251 9838.

Ireland Ankara: Ugur Mumcu Caddesi 88, MNG Binasi Bloc, kat 3, Gaziomanpaşa. *Tel: (312) 446 6172.*
Istanbul: Acisu Sokak 5, d4, Macka.
Tel: (212) 259 6979.

United States of America Ankara: Kavaklıdere, Atatürk Bulvarı No 110.
Tel: (312) 455 5555;
www.usemb-ankara.org.tr
Istanbul: Kaplicalar Mevki Sokak 2, Istinya. *Tel: (212) 335 9000.*
Izmir: *Tel: (232) 464 8755.*
Adana: *Tel: (322) 346 6262.*

United Kingdom Ankara: Çankaya, Sehit Ersan Caddesi No 46/A.
Tel: (312) 455 3344;
www.britishembassy.org.tr
Istanbul: Mesrutiyet Cad 34, Tepebasi, Beyoğlu 34435.
Tel: (212) 334 6400.
Izmir: 1442 Sokak No 49, Alsancak.
Tel: (232) 463 5151.
Antalya: 1314 Sokak 6/8, Gençlik Mahallesi. *Tel: (242) 244 5131.*
Bursa: Ressam Sefik Bursali Sokak, Basak Caddesi, Zemit Kat.
Tel: (224) 220 2534.

Emergency telephone numbers

Ambulance *112*
Police *155*
Fire *110*
In Istanbul there are also private ambulance firms.

Language

Turkish is a Ural-Altaic language, related to Finnish and Hungarian. It has been written in Latin script since 1928 when Atatürk abolished the Arabic script used by the Ottomans.

PRONUNCIATION

c = j as in 'John'; cami (mosque) = jami
ç = ch as in 'church'; Foça = Focha
ğ = soft g, unpronounced, it extends the preceding vowel as in
    dağ (mountain) = daa
ı (dotless i) = as in the initial a in 'away'. For example, Topkapı = Topkapa
ö = like the vowel sound in 'fur';
ş = sh as in 'shop'; Kuşadası = Kushadasa
ü = as in French 'tu'.

GREETINGS AND POLITENESSES

Hello	merhaba
Goodbye	güle güle (said by the one staying behind)
	allahaısmarladık (said by the one leaving)
Good morning	günaydın
Good evening	iyi akşamlar
Good night	iyi geceler
Please	lütfen
Thank you	mersi or teşekkur ederim

EVERYDAY EXPRESSIONS

Yes	evet
No	hayır or yok
There is	var
There is not	yok
I want	istiyorum
How much?	ne kadar?
Expensive	pahalı
Cheap	ucuz
Money	para
Very beautiful	çok güzel
Toilet	tuvalet
Men's (toilet)	baylar
Women's (toilet)	bayanlar

TIME

Today	bugün
Yesterday	dün
Tomorrow	yarın
What is the time?	saat kaç?

THE DAYS OF THE WEEK

Sunday	Pazar
Monday	Pazartesi
Tuesday	Salı
Wednesday	Çarşamba
Thursday	Perşembe
Friday	Cuma
Saturday	Cumartesi

NUMBERS

1	bir	8	sekiz
2	iki	9	dokuz
3	üç	10	on
4	dört	20	yirmi
5	beş	50	elli
6	altı	100	yuz
7	yedi	1000	bin

Health

There are no mandatory vaccination requirements. Immunisation against typhoid, tetanus, polio and hepatitis A is recommended. There is no malaria risk in the Mediterranean coastal regions, but east of Ankara anti-malarial tablets are recommended between March and November. Avoid swimming in fresh water near the Syrian border. AIDS is present in Turkey, as in all parts of the world. Take sensible precautions over uncooked food, and drink only bottled water.

For minor problems go to the pharmacy (*eczane*) and describe your symptoms. If necessary, your hotel will call a doctor but there will be a charge for this. If hospital treatment is needed, use the American Hospital in Nişantaşı, Istanbul (*tel: (212) 231 4050*), or the German Hospital in Taksim, Istanbul (*tel: (212) 293 2150*), or the American Hospital in Izmir (*tel: (232) 484 5360*). Treatment must be paid for, so medical insurance is essential.

When at the coast keep a careful eye out for jellyfish, which sting, and sea urchins, whose black spines should not be trodden on.

Media

Turks are avid newspaper readers and there are a great many Turkish papers. The only English-language daily is the *Turkish Daily News*. Foreign newspapers are available in the big cities one day after publication. The leading Turkish dailies are *Hürriyetim*, *Milliyet*, *Sabah*. The Voice of Turkey broadcasts in English from 7.30am–12.45pm and from 6.30–10pm on the following frequencies: 100.6MHz, 97.4MHz, 101.6MHz, 100.5MHz, 101.9MHz and 103MHz.

Money matters

The Turkish currency, the lira, has been under considerable pressure since the late 1990s and devaluations and rampant inflation caused exchange rates to go haywire. Everything cost millions of lira, even a soft drink. However, in 2005 the government introduced a Yeni (New) Turkish lira, YTL, worth the equivalent of 1 million old lira. New notes are in denominations from 1 to 100 YTL, and coins are denominated from 1 kuru to 1 YTL (a kuru is one-hundredth of a YTL). In practice, you will often be charged in euros or sterling in tourist resorts.

There is no limit on foreign currency brought into the country, but no more than US$5,000 worth of Turkish liras can be taken in or out. Keep your exchange slips to show when taking souvenirs out of the country to prove they have been purchased with legally exchanged money, or if you want to change any Turkish lira back to foreign currency. There are many banks and almost all will exchange foreign currency. Most three-star hotels and upwards offer an exchange service. Foreigners can use VISA cards to obtain local currency from cash

CONVERSION TABLE

FROM	TO	MULTIPLY BY
Inches	Centimetres	2.54
Feet	Metres	0.3048
Yards	Metres	0.9144
Miles	Kilometres	1.6090
Acres	Hectares	0.4047
Gallons	Litres	4.5460
Ounces	Grams	28.35
Pounds	Grams	453.6
Pounds	Kilograms	0.4536
Tons	Tonnes	1.0160

To convert back, for example from centimetres to inches, divide by the number in the third column.

MEN'S SUITS

UK	36	38	40	42	44	46	48
Turkey & Rest of Europe	46	48	50	52	54	56	58
USA	36	38	40	42	44	46	48

DRESS SIZES

UK	8	10	12	14	16	18
France	36	38	40	42	44	46
Italy	38	40	42	44	46	48
Turkey & Rest of Europe	34	36	38	40	42	44
USA	6	8	10	12	14	16

MEN'S SHIRTS

UK	14	14.5	15	15.5	16	16.5	17
Turkey & Rest of Europe	36	37	38	39/40	41	42	43
USA	14	14.5	15	15.5	16	16.5	17

MEN'S SHOES

UK	7	7.5	8.5	9.5	10.5	11
Turkey & Rest of Europe	41	42	43	44	45	46
USA	8	8.5	9.5	10.5	11.5	12

WOMEN'S SHOES

UK	4.5	5	5.5	6	6.5	7
Turkey & Rest of Europe	38	38	39	39	40	41
USA	6	6.5	7	7.5	8	8.5

dispensers at Iş Bank and Yapı-Kredi Bank (the latter also accepts Eurocard and MasterCard).

There is a free foreign exchange market. Prices follow Central Bank exchange quotations and are printed in the *Turkish Daily News*.

Credit cards are widely accepted. Traveller's cheques are easily exchanged in banks and at hotels. Sterling and US dollar traveller's cheques are recommended. Except in the larger hotels, it is not usually possible to settle bills directly with traveller's cheques.

National holidays
Official

1 January New Year's Day

23 April National Sovereignty and Children's Day

19 May Atatürk's Commemoration and Youth and Sports Day

30 August Victory Day

29 October Republic Day

Government offices and businesses shut on these days, but shops remain open.

Religious

There are two major Muslim festivals. The Feast after Ramadan, celebrating the end of fasting, is a three-day national holiday. The Feast of the Sacrifice, celebrating Abraham's willingness to sacrifice his son, is a four-day national holiday. All hotels on the coast are full and all offices shut. The dates for these festivals follow the lunar calendar and therefore move backwards by 11 days each year.

Opening hours

Banks Mon–Fri 8.30am–noon & 1.30–5pm.

Shops Mon–Sat 9am–7pm.

Museums Winter 8.30am–noon & 1.30–5pm; summer 8.30am–5.30pm. Closed: Mon. Except the Topkapı Palace which is closed Tue.

Government offices Mon–Fri 8.30am–12.30pm & 1.30–5.30pm.

Organised tours

There are numerous organised tours in Turkey. They operate from Istanbul and the major resorts. Try **Jasminne Tours**, Akbıyık Caddesi 61, Sultanahmet *tel: (212) 638 0276; fax: (212) 638 1283; www.jasminnetours.com*).

Pharmacies

Pharmacists in Turkey are highly qualified, and can take your blood pressure and give injections. Most non-addictive drugs and medicines can be bought without a prescription. Each district in large cities like Istanbul and Ankara has a pharmacy open 24 hours a day. The name of the duty pharmacy is listed in all the other pharmacies. Normal opening hours are Monday to Saturday 9am–7pm.

Places of worship

As well as the mosques for Muslim worship on most street corners, Istanbul has the Catholic San Antonio di Padova on Istiklal Caddesi, Beyoğlu, and the Anglican Saint Helena's Chapel at the British Consulate, Tepebaşı, and the Neve Shalom synagogue on Büyük Hendek Caddesi, Şişhane. The synagogue in Istanbul was damaged by a bomb blast in November 2003. It would be advisable to consult with the religious authorities in your own country as to when it will be open again and the security measures in place there.

Police

Tourist police are there to help tourists in the event of crime and are easily recognisable by their beige uniforms and maroon berets (**Istanbul** *tel: (212) 527 4503/528 5369;* **Ankara** *tel: (312) 384 0606;* **Izmir** *tel: (232) 446 1454*). They also have offices in all towns throughout the country. Traffic police wear green uniforms and white caps, while market police in blue uniforms patrol the markets and bazaars to check commercial practice. The *Jandarmas* (gendarmerie) are soldiers in green army uniform with a red armband who keep the peace, prevent smuggling, etc.

Post offices

Turkish post offices are easily recognisable by their yellow PTT signs. In Istanbul and Ankara the main post offices are open 24 hours a day, while smaller ones throughout the country share government office hours. Poste restante letters should be addressed 'poste restante' to the central post offices (*Merkez Postanesi*) in the town of your choice. Proof of identity is required on collecting poste restante.

Public transport

Details of trains, buses and ferries are in the *Thomas Cook Overseas Timetable*, published bimonthly and obtainable from Thomas Cook branches in the UK or *tel: 01733 416477*.

By air

Turkish Airlines (THY) (*www.turkishairlines.com*) operates internal flights between Ankara, Istanbul, Izmir, Adana, Antalya, Dalaman, Milas/Bodrum, Elazığ, Diyarbakır, Erzurum, Gaziantep, Kayseri, Konya, Malatya, Trabzon and Van. THY has ticket reservation offices in all major cities. The main offices are in **Istanbul** (*tel: 247 1338; fax: 240 2984*) and **Ankara** (*tel: 398 0100; fax: 398 0336*).

By bus

This is the best way to travel the smaller distances that do not require flying. The coaches are comfortable, air-conditioned, no-smoking, and the service is inexpensive, efficient and reliable. Coaches/buses depart from bus stations, *otogar*, and seats should be booked a day or two in advance either at the local bus station or at a travel agent.

By ferry

Turkish Maritime Lines (TML Central Office, Rıhtım Caddesi, Merkez Han 4, Karaköy; *tel: (212) 249 7178; fax: (212) 251 9025; www.tdi.com.tr*) run a car ferry from Istanbul to Izmir, Marmaris and Mersin, three times a week. TML also run a Black Sea line departing Mondays from Istanbul to Trabzon, calling at Sinop, Samsun, Ordu and Giresun, from May to October. Ferries from Istanbul and other ports across the Bosporus are frequent and very cheap. Brass tokens are used as tickets, bought at the quayside. All Bosporus ferries depart from the three quays beside the Galata Bridge.

By taxi

Dolmuş taxis are the cheapest. These zippy minibuses run along specified routes and can be flagged down anywhere along the route. Normal taxis are metered and reasonable, the best way to travel in cities.

By train

Trains have first- and second-class seating, and some have restaurants and

Tram at Taksim Square, Istanbul

eeping cars. On the European side, rains from Edirne and Greece arrive at irkeci Station near Eminönü Square, while on the Asian side trains depart om Haydarpaşa Station (20 minutes cross the Bosporus by ferry) to Ankara nd all points east. Tickets are bought t the station or reserved via a travel gent. The Mavi Tren (Blue Train) is ne fast intercity service, leaving Iaydarpaşa twice daily.

y tram

Vithin Istanbul there are high-speed rams running from Aksaray to erhatpaşa and Sirkeci. An old-ashioned tram still runs along stiklal Caddesi between Galata and aksim. There is also the Tünel, the vorld's oldest and shortest subway, a unicular train running from Karaköy p the hill to Beyoğlu, which has wo stations.

tudent and youth travel

Iolders of most internationally ecognised student cards are entitled o student reductions at museums and ccommodation at Turkish Youth Iostels. The main office is in Istanbul Gençtur Turizm ve Seyahat Acentasi, erebatan Cad. 15/3, Sultanahmet; el: 520 5274).

ustainable tourism

'homas Cook is a strong advocate of thical and fairly traded tourism and elieves that the travel experience hould be as good for the places visited as it is for the people who visit them. That's why we firmly support The Travel Foundation, a charity that develops solutions to help improve and protect holiday destinations, their environment, traditions and culture. To find out what you can do to make a positive difference to the places you travel to and the people who live there, please visit *www.thetravelfoundation.org.uk*

Telephones

Emergency ambulance services *112*
Directory enquiries and pharmacies on duty *118*
Long-distance operator *131*
International reverse charge calls *115*
Long-distance enquiries *161*
Cheap rates apply between 8pm and 8am. Public phones accept cards available from newspaper stands and some shops. Many phones in Istanbul and resorts will allow international direct dialling and also allow payment by credit card. Eastern Turkey does not have these facilities. Most 3-star hotels will have a direct-dial facility, but ask about call surcharges, which can be very high. Most major post offices have a facility for operator-assisted calls that you pay for on completion.

To call abroad from Turkey dial *9*, then, after a new tone, *9* again for an international line, then the country code, then the number itself. The country code for **Australia** is *61*, **Canada** is *1*, **Ireland** is *353*, **New Zealand** is *64*, **UK** is *44* and **USA** is *1*.

Time

UK and Ireland are 2 hours behind Turkey all year round. Australia and New Zealand are 8 hours ahead, while USA and Canada are 7 hours behind.

Tipping

When 10–15 per cent service charge is added to your bill, it is customary to leave an extra 5 per cent for the waiter. In smaller restaurants where service is not included, 10 per cent is normal. Taxi drivers do not expect tips. Masseuses will be delighted with a small tip. Mosque attendants can be given a tip if they have opened something specially, while shoe attendants can be left a small note.

Tourist offices

Before you go you can obtain information from

5997568; www.tourismturkey.org

Australia Level 3, Room 17, 428 George Street, Sydney NSW 2000. *Tel: (612) 9223 3055; fax: (612) 9223 3204.*

Canada Constitution Sq, 360 Albert St, Suite 801, Ottawa, Ontario K1R 7X7. *Tel: (613) 230 8654; fax: (613) 230 3683; www.turkishtourism.ca*

UK and Ireland 29–30 St James's St, London SW1A 1HB. *Tel: (020) 7839 7778; fax: (020) 7925 1388; www.gototurkey.co.uk*

USA 2525 Massachusetts Ave NW, Suite 306, Washington DC 20008. *Tel: (202) 612 6800; fax: (202) 319 7446; www.tourismturkey.org*

821 United Nations Plaza, New York, NY 10017. *Tel: (212) 687 2194; fax: (212) 5997568; www.tourismturkey.com*

Offices are all over the country and at the airports of Istanbul, Ankara, Izmir, Adana and Dalaman. At Istanbul there are additional tourist offices at the Hilton Hotel Arcade, Sultanahmet Square, Karaköy Maritime Station, and the Central Office (Meflrutiyet Caddesi 57/6, Beyoğlu; *tel: 243 3731; fax: 252 4346*).

Travellers with disabilities

Some modern museums and hotels have special facilities, but provision in much of Turkey remains inadequate or nonexistent and archaeological sites, castles and older museums present problems for people with limited mobility. Always make enquiries with the establishment concerned if you have special needs. Turkish State Railways (TCDD) make a reduction of 70 per cent for travellers with disabilities, with a 30 per cent reduction for those accompanying them. For information: Özürluler Federesyonu, Gurabba Huseyinama Caddesi, Cineirraklibostan Sokak, Mermer Ifl Hanı, Aksaray, Istanbul (*tel: (212) 534 5980*).

Useful general websites

www.gototurkey.co.uk
www.turkeytravelplanner.com
www.theguideturkey.com
www.mymerhaba.com
www.hotelguide.com.tr
www.travelguide.gen.tr

Acknowledgements

Thomas Cook wishes to thank the photographers, picture libraries and other organisations for the loan of the photographs reproduced in this book, to whom copyright in the photographs belongs.

AFP/GETTY IMAGES/Mustafa Ozer 140; ASSOCIATED MEDIA GROUP/Peter Langer 110, 111, 128, 134, 139; PETE BENNETT/Big World Publications 5, 6, 7, 11, 12b, 17, 26, 37, 38, 40, 50, 61, 69, 70, 72, 75, 77, 78, 79a, 83, 86, 87, 89, 96, 98a, 98b, 99, 103, 105, 122, 143, 147, 151, 153, 156, 159, 164, 167, 179; EXCLUSIVE ESCAPES 174 FLICKR/ex-novo 29, Fenillu 36, pizzajoevt 95, Neil Carey 125; Onopko 174; FOTOLIA/Denis Kotov 97, Kobby Dagar 109, Enver Sengul 137, Jonatha Borzicchi 145; MARY EVANS PICTURE LIBRARY 59, 126; PICTURES COLOUR LIBRARY 121, 141; SPECTRUM COLOUR LIBRARY 107, 132, 135; STOCK:XCHNG/Ephedrin 115; THOMAS COOK TOUR OPERATIONS LTD 171; WIKIMEDIA COMMONS/Innana 43, en:User:Bigdaddy1204 45; WORLD PICTURES/Photoshoot 1, 21, 24, 63, 65, 66, 67, 68, 78, 125, 163, 169, 173, 183, 185.

The remaining pictures are held in the AA PHOTO LIBRARY and were taken by DARIO MITIDIERI with the exception of pages 8, 10, 12a, 13a, 20, 23b, 25, 33, 35, 48, 80a, 81, 187 which were taken by ANTONY SOUTER.

Proofreading: JAN McCANN for CAMBRIDGE PUBLISHING MANAGEMENT LTD

SEND YOUR THOUGHTS TO
BOOKS@THOMASCOOK.COM

We're committed to providing the very best up-to-date information in our travel guides and constantly strive to make them as useful as they can be. You can help us to improve future editions by letting us have your feedback. If you've made a wonderful discovery on your travels that we don't already feature, if you'd like to inform us about recent changes to anything that we do include, or if you simply want to let us know your thoughts about this guidebook and how we can make it even better – we'd love to hear from you.

Send us ideas, discoveries and recommendations today and then look out for your valuable input in the next edition of this title. And, as an extra 'thank you' from Thomas Cook Publishing, you'll be automatically entered into our exciting prize draw.

Emails to the above address, or letters to Travellers Project Editor, Thomas Cook Publishing, PO Box 227, Coningsby Road, Peterborough PE3 8SB, UK.

Please don't forget to let us know which title your feedback refers to!